Essex

A DOG WALKER'S GUIDE

Len Banister

COUNTRYSIDE BOOKS
NEWBURY BERKSHIRE

First published 2011
© Len Banister
Reprinted 2017, 2020, 2021
Updated and reprinted 2026

All rights reserved. No reproduction
permitted without the prior permission
of the publisher:

COUNTRYSIDE BOOKS
3 Catherine Road
Newbury, Berkshire

To view our complete range of books,
please visit us at
www.countrysidebooks.co.uk

ISBN 978 1 84674 238 5

Photographs by the author

Cover photograph supplied by
Roger Evans

Designed by Peter Davies, Nautilus Design
Produced through MRM Associates, Tadley
Printed by Holywell Press, Oxford

Contents

Walk

Appendix

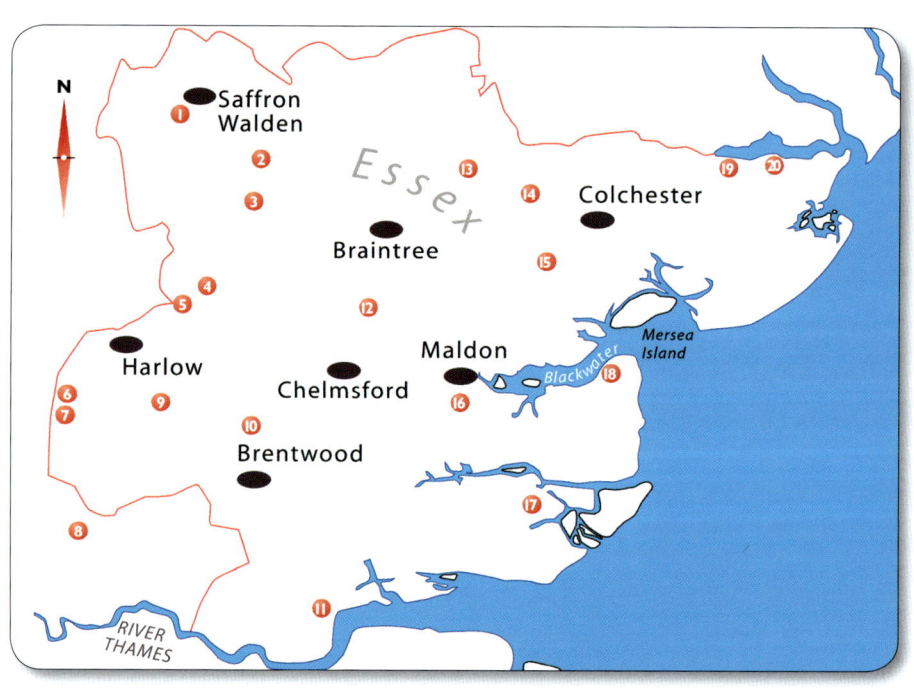

Area map showing location of the walks.

INTRODUCTION

Whilst **I am very pleased with the success** of the two previous editions of the *Dog Walker's Guide*, the time has come for a complete revision of the book. My wife, Julie, and I have re-walked all sections.

Over the last fifteen years, there have been many changes – some for the good like the replacement of stiles by gates, and some sad like the disappearance of pubs. Many car parks which were at one time free to use now require payment. People and nature have combined to alter the landscape; field edges have become hedged paths; thickets have developed into woods.

The good news is that, despite Local Authority cuts, the quality of Public Rights of Way has improved since the first edition. If you do encounter difficulties on the ground, with signage or furniture (like stiles or bridges) please report them to the Highway Authority using www.essexhighways.org/tell-us/public-rights-of-way-issues, it's also useful to contact the Ramblers who also carry out maintenance on the paths ww.essexareahub.co.uk/landing.html. In the event of other difficulties, please contact me at len@talkingwalking.co.uk.

I am still in debt to the original owners and dogs who inspired this book.

Len Banister

ADVICE FOR DOG WALKERS

'Having a dog provides a great excuse for taking a walk. The benefits of getting out and about in the fresh air with your four-legged friend are many, so enjoy the rewards and happy dog walking.' *(This and the basis for the advice that follows comes from the Natural England website: www.naturalengland.org.uk)*

As everyone knows, you must have your dog on a short lead when walking along roads. You do not have to have your dog on a lead on public footpaths but you should always do so if you cannot rely on its obedience – this is especially important on bridleways where you might meet horses and cycles; you could be liable for damages if your dog causes an accident.

If you use an extending lead, always take care near other walkers to ensure that they are not in danger of being tripped or entangled.

In the countryside the dog owner has a responsibility to avoid scaring farm animals or wildlife. From 1 March to 31 July you should keep your dog on a lead in all areas where there are likely to be breeding birds. In Essex, birds are also raised for shooting; if you see game birds, especially in late summer and autumn, you should put your dog on a lead. The routes in this book tend to avoid walks through fields with livestock but if you do encounter farm animals, put the dog on the lead.

In the case of cattle, avoid passing between cows and their calves. Cattle will sometimes show a great interest in dogs – if this becomes threatening, release the dog and leave the field by the nearest exit; the dog will move faster than the cattle and look after itself.

Always clear up after your dog wherever you are and get rid of the mess responsibly – a very small minority of owners are giving the rest a bad name by leaving their plastic bags adorning fences and trees. It is also a good idea to make sure that your dog is wormed regularly to protect it, other animals and people.

And finally, if you have bought this book, you are likely to be a dog-lover. It's worth remembering that not everyone shares your passion. Please restrain your dog near other walkers; they don't necessarily appreciate that he or she '... is just being friendly!'

PUBLISHER'S NOTE

We hope that you obtain considerable enjoyment from this book. Although at the time of publication all routes followed public rights of way or permitted paths, diversion orders can be made and permissions withdrawn.

We cannot, of course, be held responsible for such diversion orders and any inaccuracies in the text which result from these or any other changes to the routes, nor any damage which might result from walkers trespassing on private property. We are anxious though that all details covering the walks are kept up to date and would therefore welcome information from readers which would be relevant to future editions.

The simple sketch maps that accompany the walks in the book are based on notes made by the author whilst checking out the routes on the ground. For the benefit of a proper map, however, we do recommend that you purchase the relevant Ordnance Survey sheet covering your walk. The Ordnance Survey maps are widely available, especially through booksellers and local newsagents.

Saffron Walden and Audley End Park

Audley End House seen from the route.

The **highlight of this walk** is the marvellous view of Audley End House to be seen from the path in the park. Formerly a monastery, it was first converted to domestic use in the 16th century and has since undergone many changes, including the attentions of Christopher Wren, whilst Capability Brown added his unmistakable touch to the gardens. It has been a residence of Henry VIII's Chancellor and various members of the Suffolk family; it was even a holiday home of Charles II for a time. Barney, a two-year-old Lakeland terrier cross is one of those dogs who is less interested in historical features though and instead looks forward to the glorious opportunities for a romp and a spot of socialising that the park has to offer. The route then passes through the hamlet of Audley End before providing an appetizer for a potential visit to the historic town of Saffron Walden.

Terrain

The walk divides evenly between parkland and surfaced paths. There is one steepish climb and some of the paths can be muddy in winter.

Where to park

Use the large Swan Meadow car park to the north of Saffron Walden. This is a pay & display car park. (GR TL533385). **Postcode:** CB10 1DB. **OS map:** Explorer 195 Braintree & Saffron Walden.

How to get there

Leave the M11 at junction 9 for the A11; take the turning at junction 9A signposted to Saffron Walden along the B184. The car park, Swan Meadow, is on the outskirts of the town, signposted to the right.

Nearest refreshments

There are no refreshments on the route unless you decide to visit Audley End House itself, which has a self-service café. However, Saffron Walden is packed with cafés, pubs, and restaurants, the vast majority of which welcome dogs.

The Walk

● ●

❶ Leave the car park area and walk right along its service road, following signs to the Town Centre, past a roundabout and continue to a blue fingerpost signed to the Salvation Army. Go right through an arch and between almshouses. Reach a lane by the **United Reformed church** and turn right. Continue through the gates of **Audley End Park**.

❷ Take the middle of three paths on the right to go diagonally across an open meadow. Cross a bridge, which takes you on to a section of partially fenced

Dog factors

● ●

Distance: 3½ miles / 5.6 km.
Road walking: 1 mile on roads with good verges. The short diversion through the town at the end of the walk is on pavements.
Livestock: Ducks and geese along the Slade at point 2 and on the pond at point 7.
Stiles: None.
Nearest vets: Mercer & Hughes, Saffron Walden.

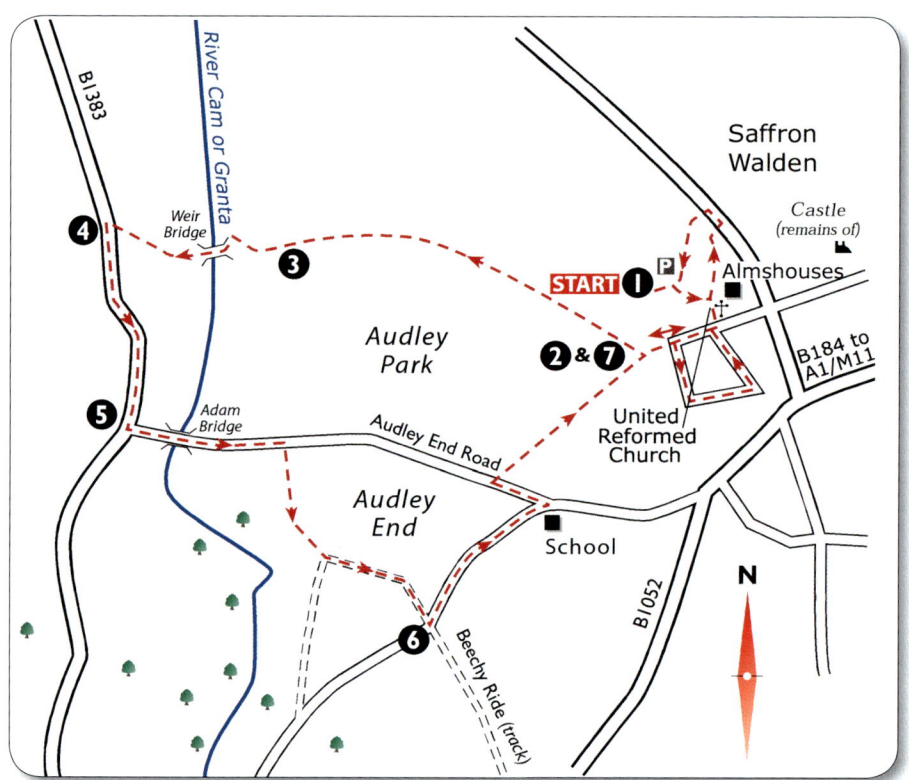

path. Keep the stream, **the Slade**, to your right and keep to the right along the edge of another meadow. (Now you should gain occasional glimpses of **Audley End House** over to the left.)

3 With a concrete bridge to your right, keep forward along a narrow path with a wall on the left and the stream on the right. (Here a dog like Barney cannot resist the temptation to leap into the water.) Join a drive and go left, still following the estate wall. This will take you up to the main road, the B1383.

4 Go left. Next to the wall is a path with a generous verge, which takes you past a gatehouse leading to stables and on to one of the iconic views of Essex: **Audley End House** with its haha and lake. Over to the left are the stables, which alone would be worth the trip to see. Continue to the road junction.

5 Turn left and walk past the children's railway on the right and the main entrance to the house. Where buildings on the right finish, go right at a white fingerpost. You are now descending the only street of the hamlet of **Audley End**; its pretty terraces were originally Jacobean almshouses. Once over the bridge at the bottom, fork left and follow the drive as it passes in front of and past farm buildings to reach a road.

8 Cross and turn left. When you reach the junction at the top of the hill, cross the road and turn left, continuing along the wall, to go through a gate on the right. Go forward, crossing a wide track, and continue in a straight line to go through the gate by which you originally entered the park.

7 Go about 70m along the road then turn right on a raised path alongside an old wall with **The Town Ditch** to the right. Near the top of the rise at the end of a wooden fence, turn left on a narrow path. At the road go left to the bottom, continuing to the left of the United Reformed church. Emerge from the almshouses; go straight across the lane, and through an arch. Fork right and walk up through a small car park and keep forward through **Myddylton Place**, passing **No 1** (which is one of the finest medieval buildings in the town), to turn left along **Bridge Street**. Take the next turning left, along **Freshwell Street**, continuing past bollards at the end to go to the right of a pond. Fork right after the bridge and return to the car park.

The splendid stables at Audley End.

2

Thaxted and the River Chelmer

Thaxted's charming guildhall.

This is the perfect short walk for both dog and owner. Almost the entire route is along wide grassy verges, which provide easy walking and plenty of running backwards and forwards for your pet.

We leave Thaxted by its church of almost cathedral proportions, with a tall spire that can be seen for miles, and soon pass a windmill, another of the town's icons. From there we follow the banks of the juvenile River Chelmer as it wends its way listlessly through the hamlet of Haslemere. The return route takes us through woodland paths and over pasture to emerge in the lower part of the town and enables us to walk up between some absolutely stunning medieval buildings and quaint streets, many of which still bear ancient descriptive names such as Fishmarket Street, Town Street, Orange Street, Weaverhead Lane, The Tanyard and Stoney Lane. Finally we reach the market square crowned by the remarkable guildhall. Whether or not you have visited Thaxted before, you will find it difficult to resist tarrying to wander around the houses, shops and pubs.

Terrain

There are no gradients to speak of and the paths are a tribute to the landowners who have left generous verges – even after heavy rain, most are unlikely to be muddy.

Where to park

There is a free car park in Margaret Street. This is clearly signposted from both ends of the centre of the town (GR TL611312). **Postcode:** CM6 2LE. **OS map:** Explorer 195 Braintree & Saffron Walden.

How to get there

Thaxted is on the B184, which runs between Saffron Walden (exit 9 of the M11) and Great Dunmow (reached from the A120).

Nearest refreshments

The Swan is passed near the end of the walk. Originally a coaching inn, the Swan is open all day every day from 7 am to 11 pm for food, drinks and afternoon tea. It is particularly dog friendly. ☎ 01371 830321.

Dog factors
. . . .
Distance: 3¾ miles / 5.6 km.
Road walking: Approximately 550m on pavements through the town at the end of the walk.
Livestock: None.
Stiles: None.
Nearest vets: Mercer and Hughes.

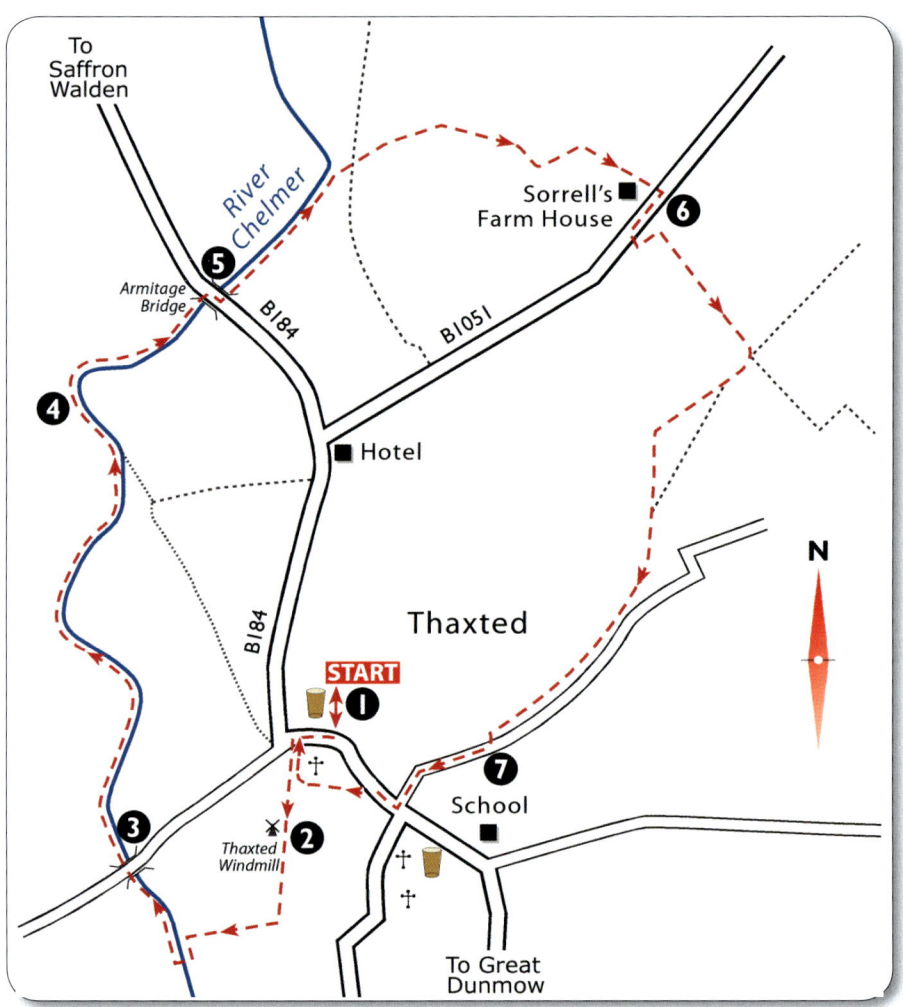

The Walk

1 Leave the car park with the lavatories to the right and go right. Go left into **Margaret Gardens**, forking right to some steps, and go left along **Bell Lane** to the main road. Turn right then cross to the main entrance of the church. Follow the path to the right, swinging left to pass between two single story houses. Follow the notice to the windmill through a gate along a terrace, going slightly right at the end through a kissing-gate, then along a hedged path, passing the windmill on the right. (Known as **John Webb's mill** and dating from the start of the 19th century, this is a tower mill, which means that the top is rotated into the wind by the 'fantail'. Restoration is taking time and the mill itself is no longer open to the public, but its grounds make an excellent picnic area.

② Keep forward along the left edge of the field then go right on a well-defined cross-track with the hedge to the right. At the bottom of the field go left then right over a concrete bridge to cross the **River Chelmer**. Immediately turn right along the field edge, with the river, which is not much more than a stream at this stage, to your right. At the end, go through a narrow gap in the hedge and over a plank bridge to a road.

③ Cross to continue with the Chelmer to your right and a pumping station on the left. After two fields keep forward over another plank bridge. After hugging the edge of quite a large field, enter a smaller one. Ignore the footbridge over to the right and keep forward over a cross-track, swinging right to rejoin the bank of the river. Keep forward with telephone poles and pylons to the left and glimpses of an attractive garden on the right. At the end of this field, swing left. Ignore a footbridge to the right and continue up the field edge to a waymarker where you turn right down to a concrete track.

④ Go left. Keep forward at the next waymarker, leaving the concrete, then, a few yards later, go right at another (labelled **Turpin's Trail**) to join another wide grassy field edge with the hedge on your right and again following the River Chelmer. Reach a road.

⑤ Go right across the river then left on a drive towards **Goddards Farm**. Soon fork left, leaving the drive at a waymarker post, now on a wide verge with trees and the river to the left. Just after the path and the river turn sharply left, you come to another waymarker; here turn right across the field to continue on a farm track, which goes up a bank. At the next field boundary turn right to walk up the field with the hedge to the left, going left at the corner to join a banked path. Climb past houses to reach a drive where you go left, passing **The Barn**, to a road.

⑥ Turn right. At a wood, opposite a pylon, go left past a barrier along a track. Soon go left over a plank bridge to walk with the hedge on the right. The path swings right along the right edge of a long narrow field. At the end, go right over a plank bridge. Don't cross the narrow field ahead but continue to the right alongside the hedge. Eventually, at a waymarker, swing sharp left to approach a wood. Just before it, go right over an earth bridge and go right back on yourself to walk with the hedge to your right. At the end of this section ignore the turn to the left and keep forward going over the left of two railed bridges. You now continue on a path to the left of a stream. When you approach houses, go straight across a meadow to go left past a gate to a drive.

7 Turn right. At the end veer left, then forward towards Thaxted Pharmacy and the main road. Go right (pass Gustav Holst's house on the left) to the right of the Guildhall, up a narrow street (passing **Dick Turpin's cottage** on the left). Continue up the hill to enter the churchyard. At the top, curve right to the road and go right to turn left at a 'No entry' sign. Go right at the end of the lane back to the car park.

Delightful cottages near the start of the walk.

Little Easton

Walking towards the stables at Brookend Farm.

This varied walk has lakes, streams, woodland and long empty fields – just the job for an energetic dog. Besides the delights of the Manor and Easton Lodge, you will walk across some open land that was once an airfield housing American bombers – you will see remnants of the airfield and, in the local church, a commemorative window.

Many of the houses on this walk bear the prominent initial M or W, which signify the historic estates of Henry Maynard, one of Henry VIII's most efficient destroyers of church property, and the Warwicks. The Countess of Warwick was described by a 1912 article in an American magazine as having 'socialistic convictions and ... so brilliantly unconventional that she has ... been the most criticised woman in the Empire'. By all accounts the Countess was extremely popular locally and had a wide circle of friends – many of whom, including H.G. Wells and Gustav Holst, lodged in her properties. Opposite the Manor you will pass a barn that she converted to a theatre.

Terrain

This is a gentle walk with few gradients, and it generally sticks to field edge paths or extraordinarily quiet country lanes. Expect some mud in wintertime.

Where to park

You are welcome to park in the Stag's car park in Duck Street if you intend to have a drink or meal there (GR TL608242). Let the landlord know of your intention. **Postcode:** CM6 2GW. Just north of the pub is Butchers Pasture where roadside parking is usually available. **Postcode:** CM6 2HY. **OS map:** Explorer 195 Braintree & Saffron Walden.

How to get there

Little Easton is on a side loop off the B184, which runs between Saffron Walden (exit 9 of the M11) and Great Dunmow (reached from the A120).

Nearest refreshments

The walk starts from the car park of the Stag www.thestaglittleeaston.co.uk; dogs are welcomed enthusiastically in the public bar. There is a whole range of good pub food available here, including a selection of sandwiches, which can be washed down by one of two well kept real ales. ☎ 01371 870214.

The Walk

● ●

❶ Leave the **Stag pub** car park, turning left. As the road curves to the left downhill, cross over right to the entrance of **White Gables** and go sharp right on a narrow-fenced path alongside the house. Keep forward with a fence to the right and, then a field where this ends, go through a gate and continue along the bottom edge of a large garden, soon with a pond to the left. Go through a gate and turn left, soon forking right in the field to head towards **Little Easton Manor**. Continue between the buildings. The **Manor House**

Dog factors

Distance: 5½ miles / 9 km.
Road walking: About 1½ miles but this is mainly along very quiet lanes.
Livestock: Horses in one field and the possibility of cattle in another.
Stiles: 6, all easily accessible to dogs, except for one that requires a little agility at the end of stage 3.
Nearest vets: Mercer & Hughes, Great Dunmow.

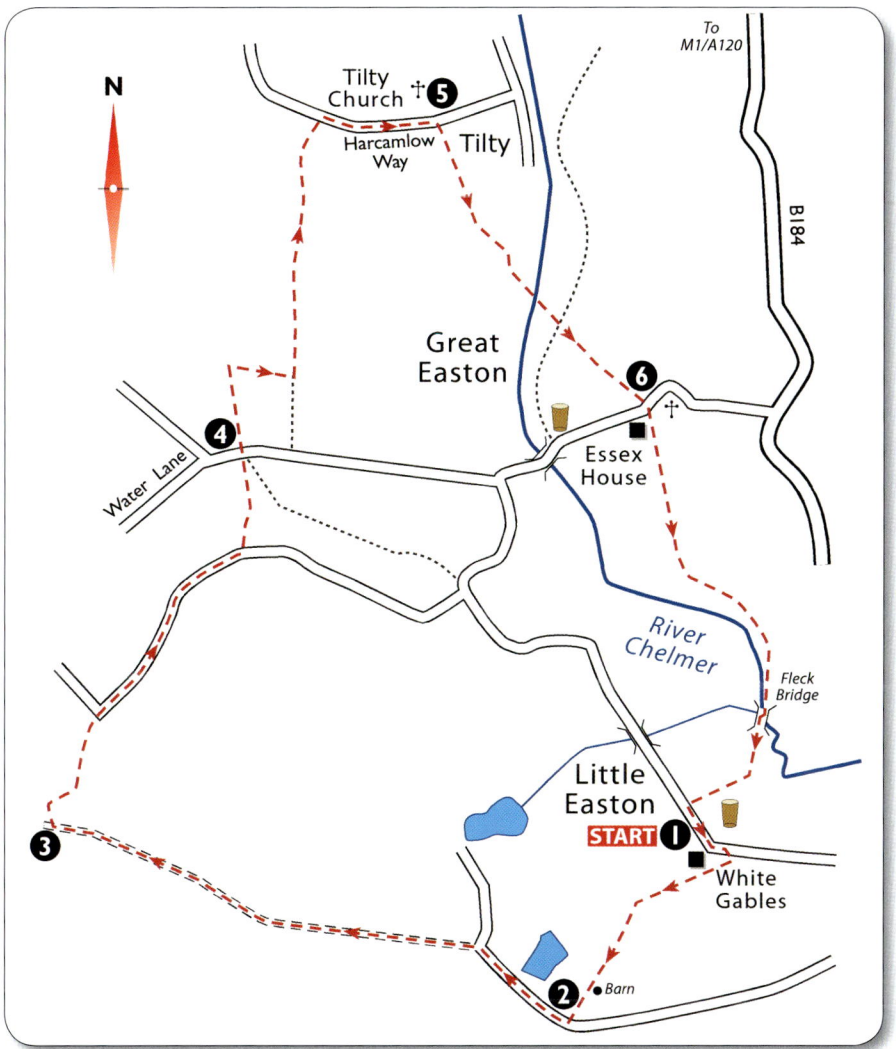

to the right is a 1930s reconstruction but the barn to the left, which houses a theatre, is genuinely old. Also on the left is a teashop which sells a range of hot meals and opposite are gardens which are open to visitors (free). Keep forward to leave by the gilded side-gate and walk up to a road. To your left is **Little Easton church**, which contains some 15th-century wall paintings representing the Passion Cycle; you can also see a memorial to the actress

Dame Ellen Terry and a stained-glass window in memory of the 386th Bomb Group USAAF, which was stationed nearby during the Second World War.

2 Go right between wooden pillars on the drive to the gardens of **Easton Lodge**. You will pass between two gorgeous lakes and continue on the drive out into open countryside. It can be of little surprise that the Americans chose this area as their air base and, as you walk along, you will notice the remains of concrete taxiing strips, brick service buildings, and hangars. Keep forward for about a mile. Diagonally left you should be able to see Stansted Airport, the proposed expansion of which would have blighted this area. (The gardens to the right are well worth visiting in early spring to see the snowdrops.) Pass Easton Lodge with its striking water-tower. Eventually reach the sign for **Brookend Farm.**

3 Turn right with the waymarker and keep forward; there are smart stables to your left. Reaching a yard, veer towards the right to join a fenced path. When you come to a tree, swing left; don't enter the field but go right along its edge with a fence to your left. This path is often quite overgrown – persist with it, it's only a short section, to arrive at a T-junction and go right. Reach a very quiet sunken lane and go right, this is now the **Harcamlow Way**. Continue for 300m and, just before a well-trimmed conifer hedge at **Cherith House**, turn left at a fingerpost along the right edge of a field to find a bridge down in the corner. Make your way up the left edge of the field, swing left at the top to go left of a gate to a road.

4 Cross diagonally left, starting on the right edge of a field and continuing forward. About halfway up, the path swings right then left to resume its direction. Now keep forward, crossing a ditch, field boundaries and a fence on the right to continue uphill to reach a brick pill box. Swing right with a hedge to reach a lane. Go right. Make a short diversion to **Tilty church** on the left. It is very simple inside although the eastern end is what remains of a vast abbey that used to occupy this site – a drawing of the original abbey can be seen inside the church porch.

5 Retrace your steps and cross the lane to follow the fingerpost across the field towards a gap in the hedge. Cross the first of several stiles which Katy, our 13-year-old black Labrador, managed much more elegantly than her owners. Now go diagonally to a stile in the corner. Join a lane and go right for 20m before going left over a stile. Cross a field, going diagonally right to a bridge over the **River Chelmer**. Continue, slightly right to cross a second bridge. Now go up the hill aiming for the middle of the hedge on the right, here cross a stile and and keep forward towards the houses of **Great Easton**. Find a stile in the corner and follow a narrow path to the road with the church to your left.

6 Cross diagonally right to go left of the beamed **Essex House** to join a narrow path between **Cottage by the Green** and a picket fence. Once in the field go forward with a wooden fence on the left, crossing a bridge at the bottom. Keep forward, almost along the line of telephone poles, to a plank bridge. Continue to the field boundary and swing left, cross a stile and follow the field boundary to find a bridge on the right. Cross this and go left to a second bridge then forward along an old field boundary. Cross a bridge and go forward uphill between fences. Once through a gate, continue up a drive through a small housing estate to reach the main road and turn left to the **Stag pub**.

The water tower at Easton Lodge bears the Warwick monogram.

4

Hatfield Broad Oak

The route to Pincey Brook.

This **walk takes you** immediately out into the countryside, with a run for your dog straight from the car park and down the only hill on the route. It then continues along the bubbling Pincey Brook. Later by a series of quiet lanes and lush field edges you pass through some fascinating, tiny, communities with beautiful houses, to be led back to the village and through the churchyard.

It is hard to believe that, at one time, Hatfield Broad Oak was one of the largest market towns in the county. The dissolution of the local Benedictine priory, the development of new roads, leading to fewer coaches a few centuries ago, and the modern bypasses have all led to the diminution in the village's importance. Luckily, many of the buildings from previous eras remain and this is what makes the lively community so attractive to the visitor. Hopefully, at the end of the walk you will spend time roaming around the village and even purchase some of the sausages that are now a famous local product.

Terrain

This is a walk of field edges and quiet lanes. There are no gradients to speak of and most of the paths are fairly mud free throughout the year – even so our terrible trio: Lizzie, an 8-year-old Jack Russell, Hattie, a 9-year-old Jack Russell mix, and the old man, Roma, a 13-year-old border terrier, all managed to get pretty filthy on our outing.

Where to park

To the left of the Cock Inn and Broad Oak stores there is a dead-end road – a little way up here is the parking area (GR TL 546166) **Postcode:** CM22 7HD. **OS map:** Explorer 183 Chelmsford & The Rodings.

How to get there

Take the B183 from Harlow or leave the M11 at junction 8 and take the B1256, which runs between Takeley and Great Dunmow; turnings from this are signposted to Hatfield Broad Oak.

Nearest refreshments

The Cock Inn is at the start of the walk; a brick built pub with a coaching arch. Whilst you can always use the road-side benches in front of the pub, dogs are only welcome at the far end of the bar; they are not allowed in the restaurant area when food is being served. ☎ 01279 718306. www. thecockinn-hatfieldbroadoak.co.uk. Towards the end of the walk you pass the Dukes Head. ☎ 01279 718598. www.thedukeshead.co.uk. Dogs are allowed in the bar area here – there is even a jar of dog biscuits to greet them. Closed on Mondays.

The Walk

• •

1 Leave the parking area alongside a concrete fingerpost, through a kissing gate,

Dog factors

• •

Distance: 4½ miles / 7 km.
Road walking: There is about ¾ mile on almost traffic-free lanes and ¼ mile at the end of the walk through Hatfield Broad Oak along a pavement.
Livestock: None, except for game birds.
Stiles: None.
Nearest vets: Bishop's Stortford Veterinary Hospital.

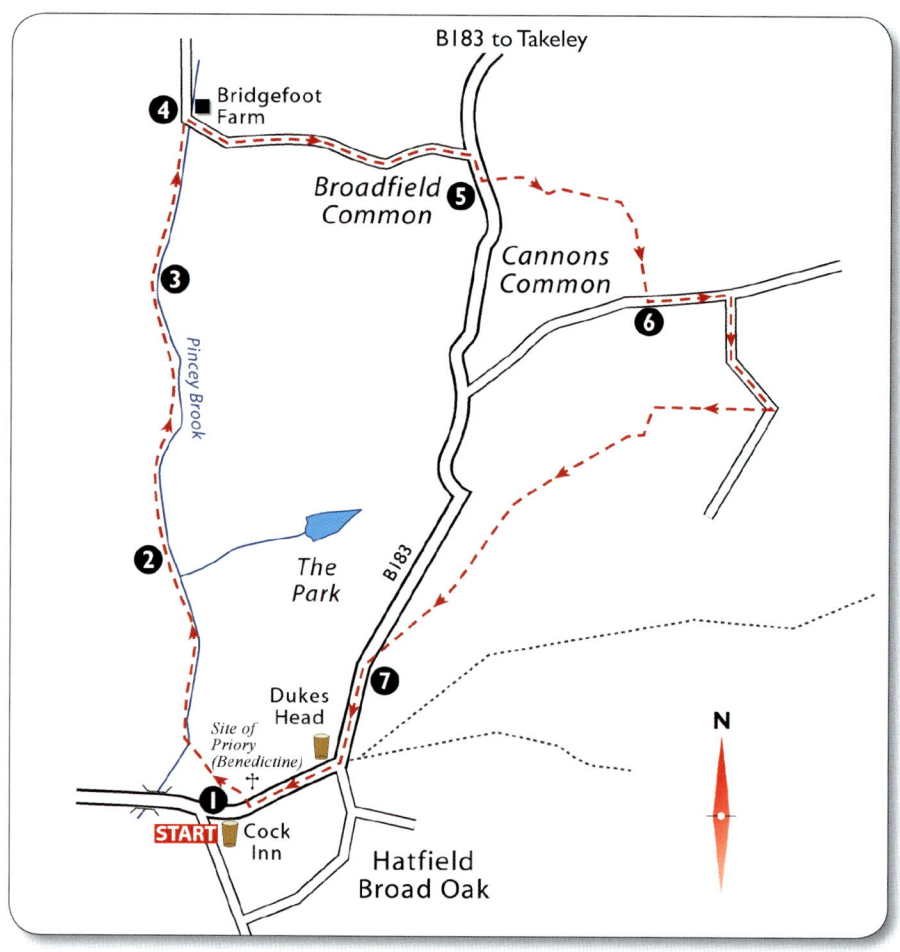

to descend, slightly to the right, down a hill. Cross a bridge and go right alongside a hedge. You will need to have your dog on a lead for this part of the walk as it runs along a conservation area to the left and the **Pincey Brook** to the right. Some boughs along the path will cause you to duck.

2 After ½ mile, cross a concrete bridge and keep forward, still alongside the brook on the right field edge. This area is prone to flooding in wintertime and, as a result, attracts a lot of waterfowl – the path, however, always remains relatively dry. In the following field continue along the right edge. A tributary of the brook will be coming in from the left and you cross this at a bridge and turn right.

3 Keep to the right-hand edge of the following two meadows – you have left the conservation area so you can let your dog off the lead but, beware, game birds are raised here and may be about in the autumn. Eventually go past a seven-bar metal gate to a lane.

4 Turn right, crossing the Pincey Brook. Go past **Collier Street Stables** and continue to a road junction. Go right then, immediately after a long shed, go left.

5 Initially you have a wooden fence on the left, and then you follow the field edge, ignoring a gap to the left. On reaching the boundary go left at a concrete post, through a small copse, turning right at a second post to follow a field edge with the hedge on your right. Swing right with the hedge, then left and, after a few metres, cross an earth bridge on the right into another field. Go straight across this to a fingerpost and lane.

6 Go left. At the first junction go right to pass through the tiny community of **Taverners Green**. Go past **Benningtons**, with its magnificent barn and, as the road swings to the right, go right through the hedge at a concrete fingerpost and across a plank bridge. Now walk along the right edge of a field. Keep with this edge as it swings left then right. At the next boundary keep forward through a gap but this time go to the right of the hedge, maintaining your direction, along a broad grassy band. You will no doubt have noticed that you are getting closer to the road over to the right. When you reach a thatched house, turn right before it to the road.

7 Turn left along the road to soon reach a pavement. Swing right with the main road past the **Duke's Head**. Go right up to the church entrance and turn left in front to continue along the shingle path to a low-lying, wood-clad building to turn right to the parking area.

Crossing the bridge over the brook.

Hatfield Heath

The 'classic' view of Matching.

The joy of this walk is the space it provides for the well-behaved dog to be let off the lead. Velvet, a Jack Russell/border collie cross, particularly enjoyed the fields, which have wide headlands, and the attractive meadows without stock. Lakes and hedged lanes provide further attractions. For the walker Hatfield Heath is always a pleasure with its green, so expansive it is almost impossible to see across. But this walk has a great deal more – it is sprinkled with gorgeous farmhouses built over the last five centuries and, halfway round, you are offered one of the cherished views of Essex in the hamlet of Matching. No wonder so many artists set up their easels here.

Terrain
This walk is relatively level. The paths can become muddy in wintertime.

Where to park
The entrance to the car park is blue signed, down an alley, off the main road, to the right of the Co-op (GR TL525150) **Postcode:** CH22 7FA. **OS map:** Explorer 183 Chelmsford & The Rodings.

How to get there
Hatfield Heath is on the A1060, which runs between Bishop's Stortford and Chelmsford. If travelling from Harlow, it is best to use the B183.

Nearest refreshments
The White Horse Inn faces the green and is near the parking place. Dogs are welcome in the small bar and the garden. ☎ 01279 730351. No food is served on Mondays. The Village Tea Rooms is also near to the parking place but does not allow dogs inside. Here you can have a very civilised tea, with toasted sandwiches and cakes. ☎ 01279 739253.

The Walk
· ·

1 Leave the car park and go right, walking across the green to the left of the church. Once alongside the church, go left and then right to continue along the main road. Opposite a road junction, cross the road and take the left of two paths alongside **Blaisdon Lodge**. This wide path soon forks; go right to

Dog factors
· ·
Distance: 6 miles / 9.6 km.
Road walking: There is a ¼ mile section at the start of stage 3 that, although it is on the Stort Valley Way, has no verges. It is fairly quiet but is used by large farm vehicles, which might frighten dogs of a nervous disposition. Quiet lanes are used extensively.
Livestock: None.
Stiles: 2; one, during stage 3, could cause a problem for large arthritic dogs.
Nearest vets: Companion Care Veterinary Surgery Pets at Home, Harlow.

pick up a right field edge, which soon swings left and crosses a field boundary so that you are now walking with a ditch on the left. At the next junction of boundaries go right and soon left alongside a ditch. Now look for steps and a bridge on the right.

2 Walk up the field with a ditch to your right. Where the field boundary goes right, cross a bridge and carry straight on across the field. (If the field has been

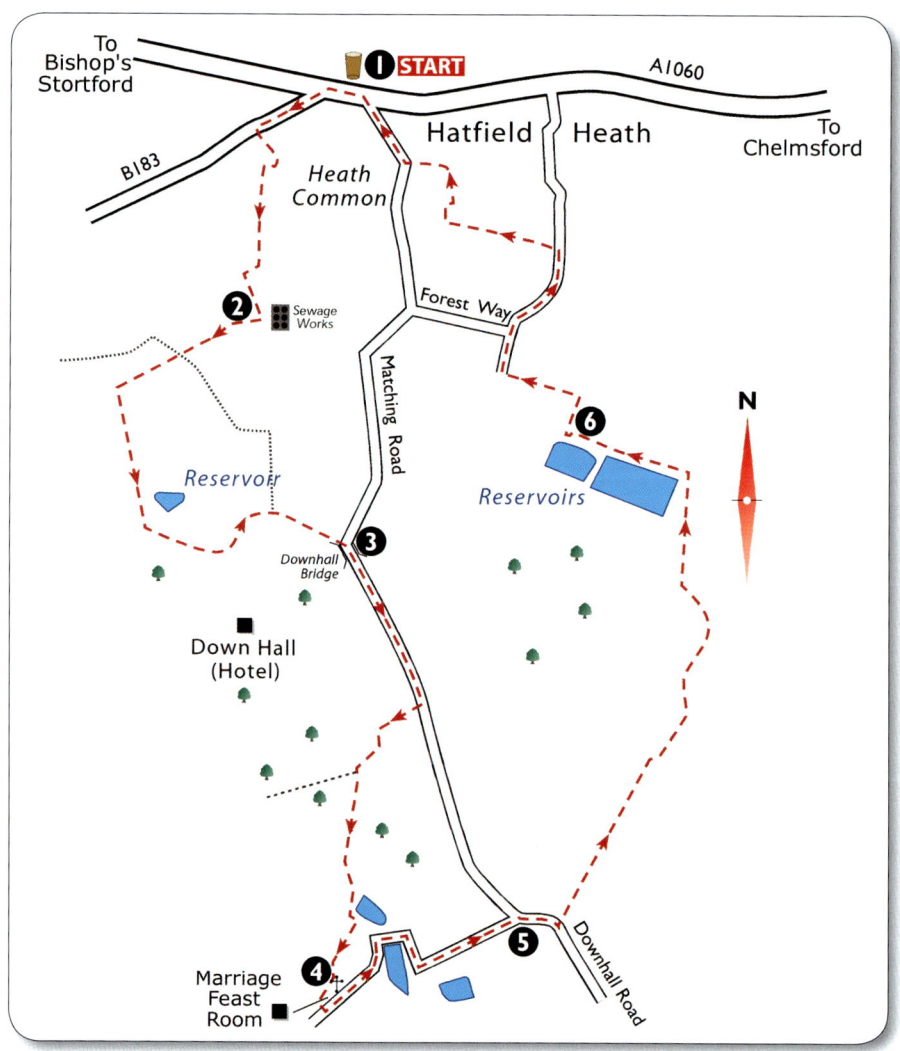

Approaching Parvilles Farm.

cropped over, the farmer may have left 'tram lines' nearby.) Reach a farm track and turn left. Pass a reservoir, at the bottom of a slope turn left with trees and the **Pincey Brook** on your right. Eventually go right past two tractor tyres to reach a road at **Downhall Bridge**.

3 Go right uphill (this road is fairly quiet but there are no verges so you need to take care that you are facing oncoming traffic, unless there is a right-hand bend ahead). Just past the bottom of the hill turn right at the second gap to go straight across the field to a stile and bridge. Just after the corner, go right through a hedge and over a stile. Now keep forward, aided by waymarkers, to reach the edge of a wood and continue alongside it. Go through a double gate into the next meadow, ignoring a gate on the right. At the bank of a reservoir turn right, following it left and, almost immediately, going right through a gap and walking up the field with a ditch on your left to a footbridge. Once across, go diagonally right to go through a gate into a churchyard.

4 Go anti-clockwise round the church, passing to the right of the **Marriage Feast Room**, which has a toilet, to reach a drive. Turn left. Now you have one of the iconic views of Essex: the church in the centre, the Feast Room to the left and a huge oak tree, planted to commemorate Victoria's Jubilee in 1887. Follow the drive round to the left, passing **Matching Farm** on the right. Pass by a lake and follow the drive as it turns right then left to a junction.

5 Turn right, then left at the next junction down the drive to **Kingstons Farm**. When this drive swings right at a concrete stand, keep forward along an attractive hedged byway, which can be muddy in wintertime. When you reach **Parvilles Farm**, go left and right between spectacular buildings to continue forward on a farm track. Join the bank of a reservoir and stay with it as it swings left to a second. At the far end, descend to cross a footbridge.

6 Turn right along the field edge. At the next boundary go left with what is left of the hedge on your right. Go right on a semi-surfaced track, which quickly develops into a drive, passing **Gibsons** on the left. Fork right at the junction. Just past a house called **Friars** set back from the road on the right, go left at a fingerpost. Follow the edge of a field with the hedge on the left. You will go right round the field and start swinging back before you reach the opening of a 'tree tunnel'. Go left here into woodland, passing benches. Eventually the path swings left then along a wooden fence to a road. Go right, crossing a junction, and keeping to the grass. Keep forward to return to the car park.

Lee Valley Park

The Lee Valley is a cornucopia of water birds and plant life.

The **Lee Valley Regional Park** stretches 26 miles / 41 km from Ware in Hertfordshire to the banks of the River Thames at East India Dock Basin. Along with Epping Forest, it supplies the major recreational destination for East London. The park's landscape ranges from rural to industrial and urban. This walk concentrates on an area that has been used for gravel extraction and landfill but has since been developed as a wonderful leisure resource. Here the River Lea Navigation runs through a complex network of streams, rivers and lakes. Unsurprisingly, waterfowl are the real stars of a day out here but the casual strips of woodland and abundant plant life provide strong supporting roles. If you have never visited the area before, this walk will hopefully whet your appetite for an early return to explore the numerous other paths you will see. This park is extraordinarily popular with dogs and their owners, and it is quite likely that you will both spend considerable time making new acquaintances.

Essex – A Dog Walker's Guide

Terrain

This is a superb year-round walk. All the path surfaces are good and you will never be troubled by mud even after the heaviest of rainstorms.

Where to park

Fishers Green free car park (GR TL377031). **Postcode:** EN9 2EE. **OS map:** Explorer 174 Epping Forest & Lee Valley.

How to get there

Fishers Green car park is approached along Stubbins Hall Lane (not Fishers Green Lane) – off a sharp corner on Holyfield Road, the B194, which runs between Broxbourne and Waltham Abbey. Follow the signposts – if the car park does not have a toilet you are in the wrong one!

Nearest refreshments

On the approach to the car park you will have passed the turning to Lee Valley Farm, an activity centre for children. This houses the Orchard Café, open daily from 10 am to 4 pm for most of the year. Here you can buy cold food, drinks and snacks – from sandwiches and wraps to salads, jacket potatoes plus treats and water for the dog. You will not be required to pay the entrance fee for the farm. ☎ 01992 892781. www.lvfarms.co.uk/visit. During the winter months you will find a variety of pubs and cafés in nearby Waltham Abbey.

The Walk

. . . .

1 Cross the road junction opposite the lavatories following the black sign to **National Grid and Lee Navigation**. Pass a picnic area on the left and cross a

Dog factors

. . . .

Distance: 4 miles / 6.4 km.
Road walking: None.
Livestock: Lots of waterfowl but well-behaved dogs can be let off the lead for all parts of the walk outside nesting time. If your dog has a serious interest in water, like Velvet, a Jack Russell/border collie cross, you might like to bear in mind that the lakes are gravel pits – as such they are deep with steep sides.
Stiles: None.
Nearest vets: Medivet, Waltham Abbey.

wide bridge over a flood relief channel. Immediately turn right beside a gate, heading for **Holyfield Weir**. This wide grassy track provides excellent riverside walking. Reach Holyfield Weir. This always provides perches for a wide variety of birds and, after heavy rain, there are spectacular torrents of water.

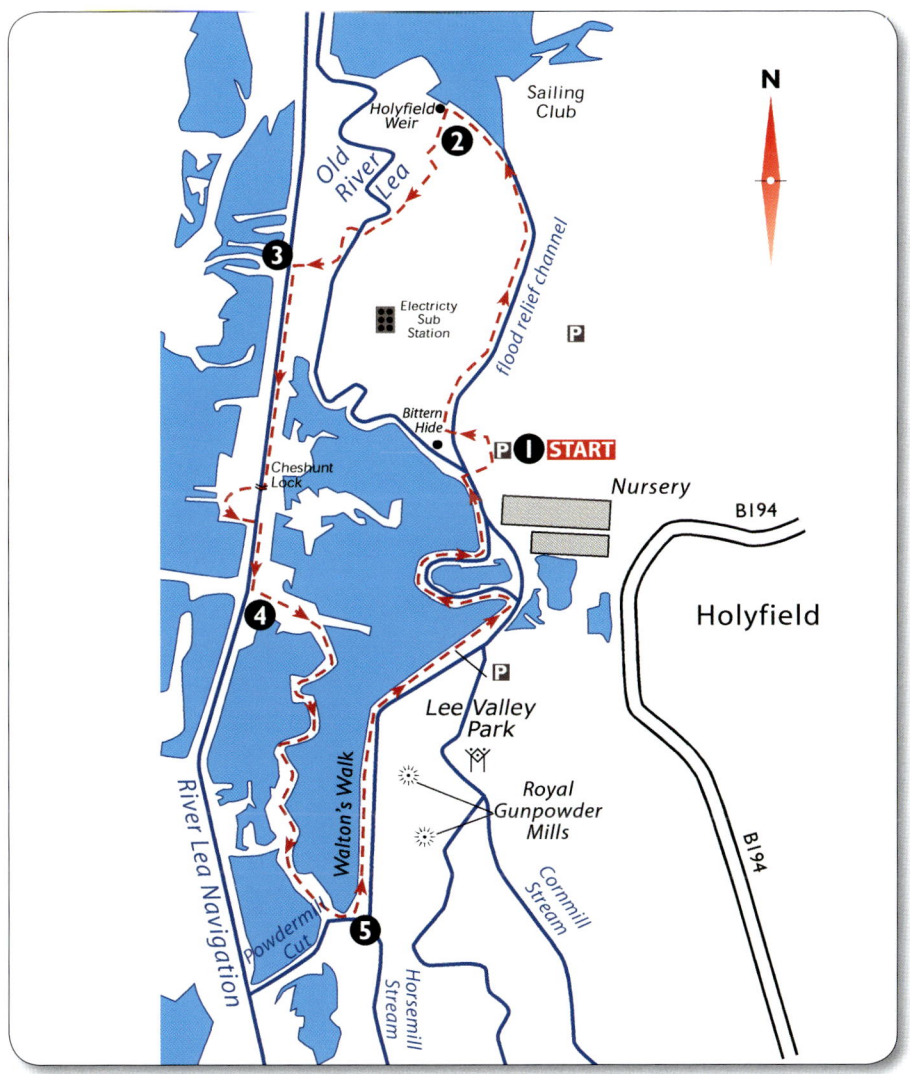

2 Exit the viewing platform for the weir, ignore the path on the right, and go straight ahead between trees. At an early T-junction, with an electricity pylon ahead, turn left to go under power lines and reach a surfaced track. Go left. Cross the **Old River Lea** by a metal bridge on the right and turn left. After about 35m, turn right at a junction and go forward over a hump-backed bridge to descend and go sharp left before a pylon. Reach a towpath.

The River Lea Navigation.

❸ Turn right to walk alongside the **River Lea Navigation** (The River Lea/Lee rises in Bedfordshire and is 58 miles long. Its last 27 miles were canalised in 1767 by the engineer John Smeaton.) When you reach **Cheshunt Lock**, fork right down a narrower path; swing left then right through a kissing gate to mount a boardwalk and follow this in a semicircle. This protected site is where, in June, one of the best displays of orchids in the London region can be seen – the most prolific is the Early Marsh, which forms a spectacular pink carpet. Leave by a second kissing gate and turn right on a path that is parallel to the towpath and enables you to see the lake to the right. Keep forward to a junction, go right up a slope then turn sharp left.

❹ Cross the bridge. Continue downhill, passing a bench on the left. About 40 yards before another bridge, go right on a much narrower path. Keep to this path as it meanders between lakes and ponds on either side. Eventually you will come to a small bridge by a tiny weir; cross it to go left at one T-junction and left again at a second, now signposted to **Fishers Green**.

❺ This broad, surfaced lane is known as **Walton's Walk** – named after Izaak Walton, the 17th-century author of *The Compleat Angler*, who enjoyed fishing here. On the right is **Horsemill Stream**. Across the stream you may be able to pick out occasional isolated buildings – these are the remains of the Royal Gunpowder Mills where, for hundreds of years, explosives were produced and, later, rocket propellants. (You can visit the site on the second and fourth Sunday throughout the year: see www.royalgunpowdermills.com/index.htm for details. Walk 7 in this book visits the Gunpowder Park, which was associated with weapons and testing.) Reach a car park and keep forward, ignoring the bridge on the right to go through a barrier. You soon follow the exaggerated meander of a river branch. Over to the left you can see platforms built for nesting and resting birds and, further over, the famous **Bittern Hide** and the rushes where the birds with their booming call are enticed to secrete themselves. Eventually you come to a bridge on the right; cross and keep forward to return to the car park.

Gunpowder Park

Grassy path through Gunpowder Park

Gunpowder Park is criss-crossed by surfaced routes with many other paths available for exploration. This short walk will hopefully introduce you and your pet to an area you will want to return to again and again – an area where you will appreciate the seasonal and long-term changes and your dog will delight in the freedom to roam over hills and down hollows.

If Capability Brown had had access to heavy earth-moving equipment he might have been engaged on projects like the Gunpowder Park. The whole of this area was, until 100 years ago, used as a testing site for weapons and explosives developed at the nearby Gunpowder Mills and the factories at Enfield Lock where the Lee Enfield rifle was developed. Contaminated earth was replaced by 100,000 cubic metres of new topsoil, which was sculptured to represent the historical activities on the site. A massive programme of planting was carried out in 2004 with the result that this 90ha/222-acre country park just gets better every year as the trees and shrubs develop.

Terrain

There are no inclines on this walk unless you choose to include some. On the outward route we use some field edge paths, which can get muddy; our return is on surfaced paths. Velvet, a Jack Russell/border collie cross, particularly enjoyed this walk as, with the exception of the Osier Marsh, she could run freely, taking advantage of the many artificial hills and the ponds formed by a recent rainstorm.

Where to park

There is a spacious car park with toilets in front of the Field Station – the latter is faced with cages containing rubble (gabions) from the original site and it's worth looking closer to see identifiable artefacts (GR TQ386994). **Postcode:** EN9 3YX. **OS map:** Explorer 174 Epping Forest & Lee Valley.

How to get there

Leave the M25 at junction 26 to join the A121 towards Waltham Abbey. Go left at the roundabout on the A112 and, almost immediately, right into the car park.

Nearest refreshments

Turn right out of the Gunpowder Park and, in ½ mile, you will reach the Plough pub on the left. Dogs are allowed in part of the pub and you are welcome to use the covered heated area outside. The Plough is part of the McMullens chain and offers a good range of food. ☎ 01992 711097. www.mcmullens.co.uk/ploughsewardstone

The Walk

. . . .

1 Walk to the left of the **Field Station** to enter the park alongside a pillar that displays every word you can think of for explosions or procedures associated with them. Walk forward past interpretation boards and take the second,

Dog factors

. . . .

Distance: 2½ miles / 4 km.
Road walking: None.
Livestock: None, except for a significant number of other dogs.
Stiles: None.
Nearest vets: Medivet, Waltham Abbey.

wider, of two turnings to the left. This region is known as '**Cob Fields** (Shock Waves Galleries)'. Go right at a T-junction. When a surfaced path curves sharply left, keep forward to a gate.

2 Turn right before the gate along a grassy path, which can get muddy. Arrive at a surfaced cross-track and go left, then swinging right. Follow this path which

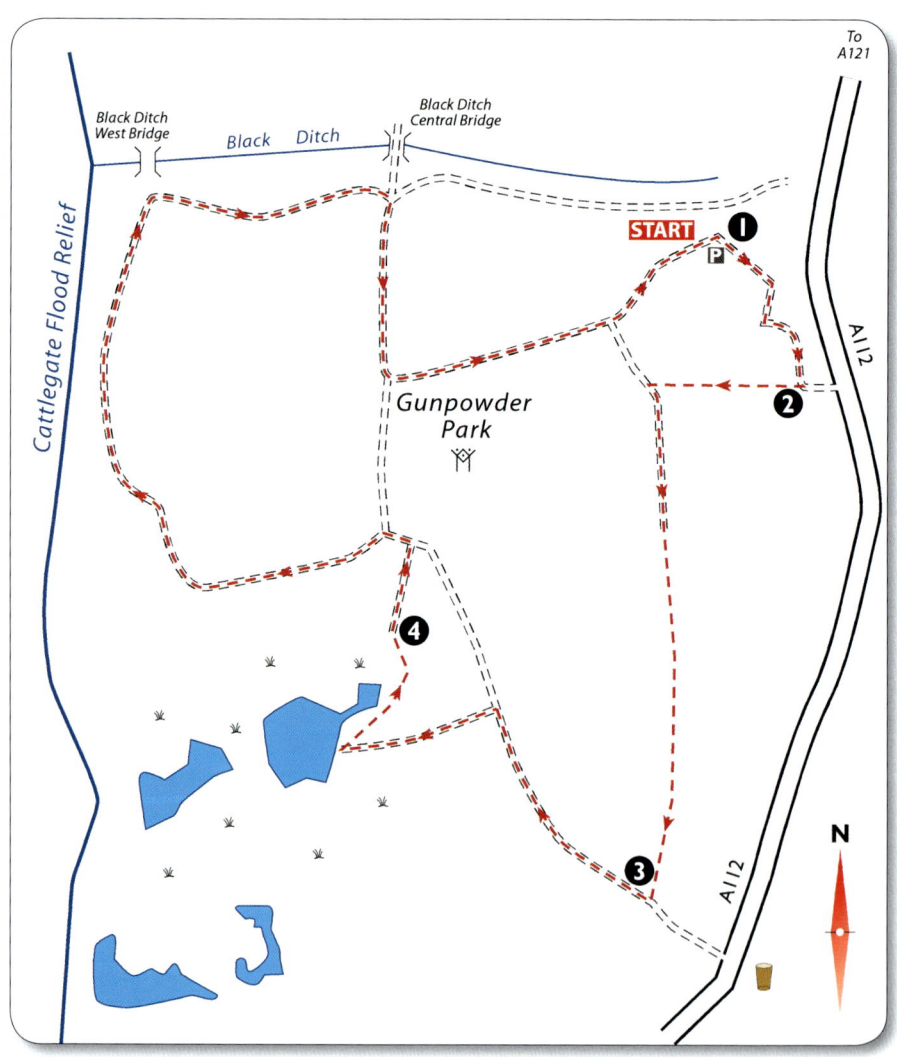

is on the **Greenwich Meridian** for about ¼ mile. This is an area known as 'The Energy Fields'. The surfaced path gives way to a grassy track then a left-hand field edge to finally cross a small concrete bridge and reach a surfaced path.

3 Go right. (If you want to visit the **Plough pub**, you should go left here and then retrace your steps.) At the first junction with waymarkers, go left, still on a surfaced track. Continue to a large hide. You are now in the midst of the **Osier Marsh**, which originally regenerated naturally and contains, amongst other trees, a variety of willow species. Retrace your steps to the first junction by an information board and turn left onto a bridge walkway. The boardwalks enable you to walk through the fallen moss-covered trees without disturbing them – here you obviously need to keep your dog on a lead. Emerge by a seat.

4 Turn right between teasels. At a T-junction, go left then left again at another T-junction. At a fork with a triangle of grass go right. (If you went left here you could visit **Enfield Island Village**, which has incorporated many of the old factory buildings and, notably, the magnificent water tower in its design.) At the next fork go right with the main path. On the right is the 'Blast Mound Plateau'. When you reach the next junction, with a bridge to a housing estate on the left, go right towards a distant line of mature trees. At the next path indicator, go left and keep to this main path to return to the **Field Station** and the car park.

One of the many surfaced paths in Gunpowder Park

Epping Forest at Walthamstow

Hollow Pond is a legacy of gravel extraction.

What a walk this is! You must take a ball or stick because your dog will want to play in each of the three great grassy areas encountered between woodland and lakes on this route. This area of Epping Forest, which is just south of the county border, is less visited than the northern sections. The main feature is the Hollow Pond, which was formed from gravel excavation in the 18th and 19th centuries. Its irregular shape, the hilly surrounds, and its several islands make it a year-round attraction for local walkers. There is more water – some of it underground in massive reservoirs and more in small ponds dotted along the route. Dogs will enjoy a swim outside nesting and young-rearing times.

The outward section of the walk takes you along Gilberts Slade (the Forest name for a glade) whilst the return is through thicker woodland, past the Italianate church of St Peter's in the Forest, and is high enough to see some extraordinary views across London.

Terrain

There are some good paths but most are likely to be muddy during the winter months and after heavy rain. However, this walk will be enjoyed so much by your dog that you shouldn't be put off by a bit of mud.

Where to park

The Boat House Car Park on Whipps Cross Road in Upper Walthamstow. This is a small car park, if it is full there is a larger one further down the road (GR TQ390886). **Postcode:** E11 1NJ.

How to get there

Whipps Cross Road is on the section of the A114 which runs between the Whips Cross and Green Man roundabouts.

Nearest refreshments

There is a tea hut that sells hot and cold drinks and simple snacks at point 6 of the route. In the busy summer period another tea hut is open near the boating area.

The Walk

. . . .

1 Walk away from the car park towards the water and turn left. Follow the path away from the road, keeping as near to the edge as is feasibly possible.

Dog factors

. . . .

Distance: 3¾ miles / 6 km.
Road walking: None, except for crossing.
Livestock: Plenty of ducks, geese and swans. Most of the wildfowl is fairly used to dogs and Velvet, a Jack Russell/border collie cross, was very well behaved in their company.
Stiles: None.
Nearest vets: Goddard Veterinary Group, Wanstead.

Essex – A Dog Walker's Guide

Eventually, arrive at a cross track with gorse in front and turn left. Keep forward over other cross tracks to continue up to a car park.

2 Cross the road. Ignore side paths. At a major junction, with a small triangle of greenery, go left. Pass a barrier to continue on the path parallel to the school road. Cross a lane and keep to the path across grass until you arrive at a road junction with traffic lights.

3 Cross the main road onto a path that, at first, runs parallel with **Forest Rise**, to eventually follow it right into woodland. Through the trees to your right you will see **St Peter's church**. Cross a surfaced track and keep forward to pass **Bulrush Pond** on the right. Ignore a heavily used path on the left. When you come to a major junction of paths with a waymarker, go left up a steep slope, which brings you to a grassy plain. Keep forward to a bridge. To your left you will have a superb view of London if the day is clear. Cross the A503.

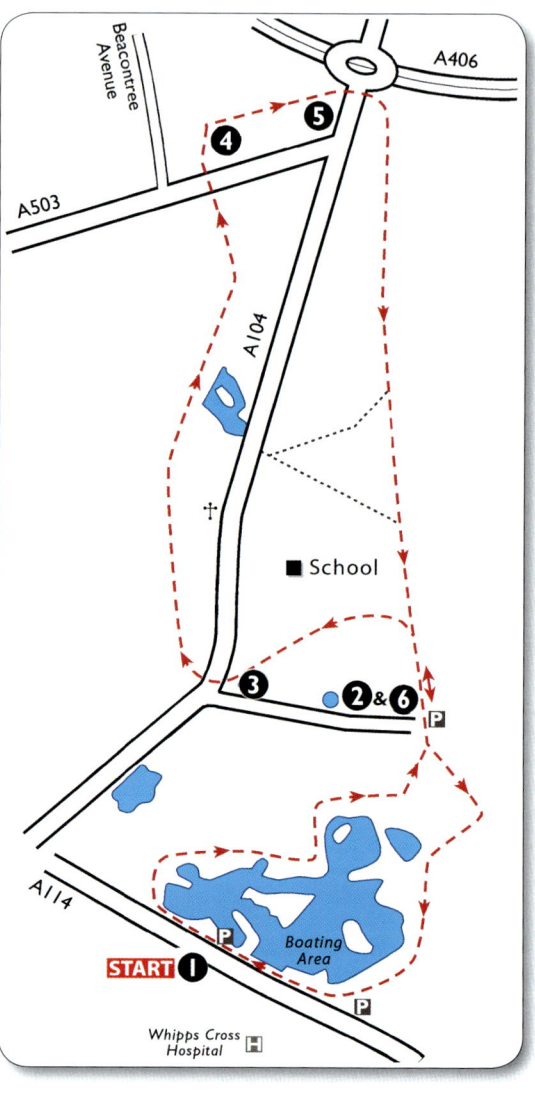

4 Go forward and turn right at a waymarker to continue through a wide gap between trees and over a bank. Cross expansive grassland, which is covering a vast cathedral-sized underground reservoir. Reach a slope to an underpass.

5 Go down, through a tunnel and right at the top. Fork right and through a second tunnel to emerge, going straight ahead across a surfaced path, on a rough track. You probably won't see them but there are rats in this area – if your dog is a ratter like Velvet, you might want to keep him/her on a lead. Keep forward on this track to eventually continue alongside the spacious **Gilberts Slade**. Further on the path swings slightly left, guided by waymarkers, eventually joining a superior track to pass a school on the right. Ignore all side paths to reach a road.

6 Cross and go through a small car park (which you may recognise from the end of stage 1), continuing to the right of an information board. Soon go right at cross tracks and then diagonally left to continue between gorse bushes which, if all has gone well, will bring you to the edge of **Hollow Pond** on your right. Now go clockwise around the edge of the pond. When you are within a few metres of the road you will see a refreshment hut near a parking area. Continue around the pond, now parallel to the road, to reach the boating area where you turn left to return to the car park.

The attractive woodland on the return route.

North Weald Bassett

The restored North Weald station.

North Weald is perhaps best known for its airfield, which opened in 1916 and which became famous in the Second World War as one of the most important and active in Essex. The airfield now houses one of the largest Saturday markets in the country.

Early on in our walk we pass the restored railway station. A group of volunteers have been working for years to reactivate the once abandoned Epping to Ongar line and you may be able to cross by a newly-installed bridge. Once away from the village we skirt arable fields to the remaining fragments of an ancient forest, to arrive at Toot Hill where you can break the outing with a quiet drink at the Green Man. The return, mainly along the Essex Way, provides good views over the countryside along paths that have been trodden for hundreds of years. Roma, a 13-year-old border terrier, thoroughly enjoys this walk on a regular basis and, just watching him, you can understand why. There are plenty of path edges to explore and fields where a dog can be safely let off the lead.

Terrain

This walk can become muddy during winter and spring. It is best undertaken on very cold days when the ground is frozen (better still when it is snow-covered) or during the summer when the paths have dried out.

Where to park

Park in the village hall car park. Visitors to the Common have half a dozen spaces allocated to them on the right-hand side – if these are occupied there is plenty of availability in nearby side roads (GR TL498040). **Postcode:** CM16 6DB. **OS maps:** The walk is covered by the margins of two maps – Explorer 183 Chelmsford & The Rodings and Explorer 174 Epping Forest & Lee Valley.

How to get there

Leave the M11 at junction 7, taking the A414 in the direction of Chipping Ongar. Turn right at the second roundabout along the B181. Follow the right-hand sign to the North Weald Bassett Village Hall from the High Road.

Nearest refreshments

Halfway round the route is the Green Man at Toot Hill. This has long been a favourite pub in the district. In the small dog-friendly bar there is a good range of beers on offer and on fine days you can take your drink and relax on the attractive forecourt, where dogs are welcome. Pub meals are available as well as an extensive restaurant menu. ☎ 01992 522255. www. thegreenmanandcourtyard.com. In North Weald and near the start of the walk is the fascinating King's Head with its maze of small rooms, three real ales and a comprehensive menu, ranging from sandwiches to grills. ☎ 01992 525001.

The Walk

. . . .

❶ Leave the car park with the village hall to your right and take a path to the right

Dog factors

. . . .
Distance: 4¼ miles / 6.8 km.
Road walking: Some very quiet lanes and about ¼ mile along roads, with pavements.
Livestock: Rarely any livestock; your dog can be off the lead for most of the time.
Stiles: 1 – quite easily passed by dogs.
Nearest vets: North Weald Veterinary Surgery.

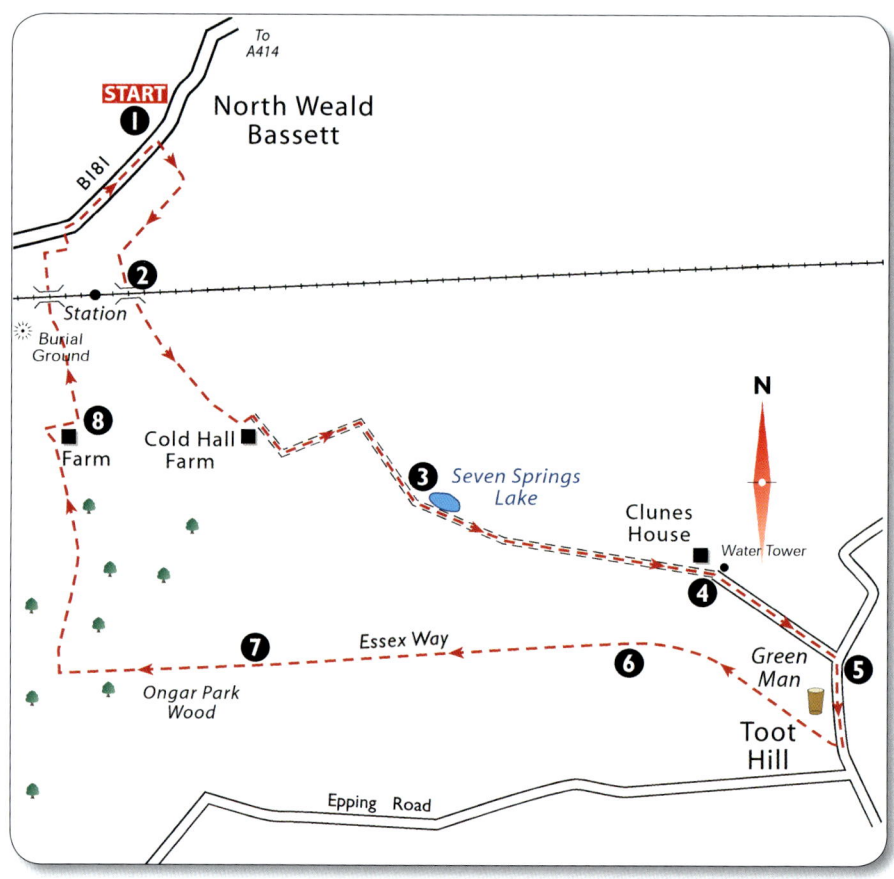

under a weeping willow onto **Weald Common**, going right with a children's play area over to the left to enter a strip of woodland. Follow a track with houses to the left and cross a road to a fence and follow a path to the left of the station.

2 Cross the railway via two gates and continue forward along the right edge of a field. At the junction, keep forward towards **Cold Hall Farm**. Pass to the left of the farm then, at the corner of the field, go left with the hedge on the right. Before a gate and old step-stile, go right along a left field edge to a wood.

3 Veer left into the wood. Almost immediately you have **Seven Springs Lake** on the left. The lake maintains its level because, as its name implies, it is fed by seven springs. The woodland is one of the remnants of an ancient forest that was destroyed in the quest for increased food production during the post-war years. The woodland walk develops into a delightful hedged path. Ignore a right fork to reach a water tower.

Ancient and modern!

④ Go forward on a quiet lane, passing **Clunes House** on the right. Reach a T-junction.

⑤ Go right, passing the **Green Man**. About 40m before a telephone box, turn right at a fingerpost to cross a stile. Follow the hedge on the right. When this swings away, keep your line to the far right-hand corner. Continue along a hedged path then, ignoring side paths, the right edge of a field. At the next boundary follow the waymarker diagonally left across the field to a gap in the hedge.

⑥ Turn left to continue on the **Essex Way** along a heavily rutted broad track which you will follow for 1 mile. After the track swaps sides with the field border you will see, over to your right, a solitary tree. This is a wild service tree that was preserved, because of its rarity, when the rest of the woodland was destroyed.

⑦ Enter **Ongar Park Wood** and keep forward, ignoring all side paths, until you cross a dry ditch and reach a major cross-track with two short barrier posts and a bank beyond. Turn right on the cross-track. This track is an ancient roadway – notice the banks on either side surmounted by trees. Eventually the track swings right to a lane by **Carisbrooke Farm**.

⑧ Turn left, pass the entrance to the **Burial Park** on the left, and go under a railway bridge. Turn right along **Waterman's Way** and go left to the main road. Turn right, passing the **King's Head**, to return to the village hall, which is on your right.

Blackmore and Birch Spring

The duck ponds at point 6 of the walk.

An early historian described Jericho Priory as: 'One of King Henry VIII's Houses of Pleasure; and disguised by the name of Jericho. So that when this lascivious Prince had a mind to be lost in the embraces of his courtesans, the cant word among his courtiers, was, that He was gone to Jericho.' It is certainly undisputed that the former house on the site of the present Jericho Priory in Blackmore was the birthplace of Henry's illegitimate son, Henry Fitzroy. The nave of the former priory still exists in the church but the latter is mainly known for its magnificent wooden steeple. Along with its historical associations, Blackmore has many of the characteristics of a picture-postcard village, with duck ponds, stocks and beautiful buildings, many of which display fine examples of pargeting – ornamental plasterwork, traditionally created using lime plaster.

This walk saves these treats for the end; having taken you through stunning woodland and wide open spaces, which will spoil any dog for variety and opportunity. I know that our trio comprising Lizzie, an 8-year-old Jack Russell, Hattie, a 9-year-old Jack Russell mix, and the old man, Roma, a 13-year-old border terrier, had a truly wonderful time racing around through woods and pastures – in fact I wouldn't be surprised to learn that Lizzie totted up 20 miles on the day.

Terrain

Mainly field edge and woodland paths, which can be muddy in wintertime.

Where to park

On Fingrith Hall Lane in Blackmore, near the crossroad and pubs (GR TL604019). **Postcode:** CM4 0RU. **OS map:** Explorer 183 Chelmsford & The Rodings.

How to get there

There are several turnings off to Blackmore from the A414, which runs from junction 7 of the M11 to Chelmsford.

Nearest refreshments

There are at least two pubs near where you park. The Leather Bottle welcomes dogs in the comfy left-hand bar. Here there are always at least four real ales on offer. Food ranges from simple sandwiches and jacket potatoes to excellent main courses. ☎ 01277 821891. www.theleatherbottle.net. Towards the end of the walk, Megarrys Tea Shop is an Aladdin's cave of antiques with a teashop attached. Here you can purchase tea of any variety, along with home-made cakes and toasted buns. It is always worth ringing beforehand to check opening times although if your party is five or six, the owner may open especially for you. Dogs are welcome on the outside shaded patio but not in the garden. ☎ 01277 821031. www.megarrysteashop.co.uk

Dog factors

Distance: 4¾ miles / 7.6 km.
Road walking: At the start there is about ½ mile of road walking, initially with a pavement, because stiles in the parallel fields are impassable for dogs.
Livestock: There may be horses in some fields and perhaps a herd of cattle.
Stiles: 5, all easily managed by dogs.
Nearest vets: House & Jackson, Blackmore.

The Walk

· ·

1 Walk away from the village for about ½ mile, along **Fingrith Hall Lane**, passing a housing estate and crossing **Redrose Lane**. Soon after passing High House on the left, go right over a bridge and through a gate up the left edge of a field.

2 Go through another gate and a short distance along the right edge of a field to a bridge. Keep to the right edge of the next field, crossing a stile to a hedged track forking left. Go through a rusty gate and between farm buildings to reach **Spriggs Lane**.

3 Turn left and after 100m turn right at a fingerpost and continue along the wide grassy right-hand edge of the field. Cross into the next field and go left alongside a ditch. Keep with this field edge to a white-topped waymarker in the far left-hand corner. Here, immediately go right of an oak over a stile and

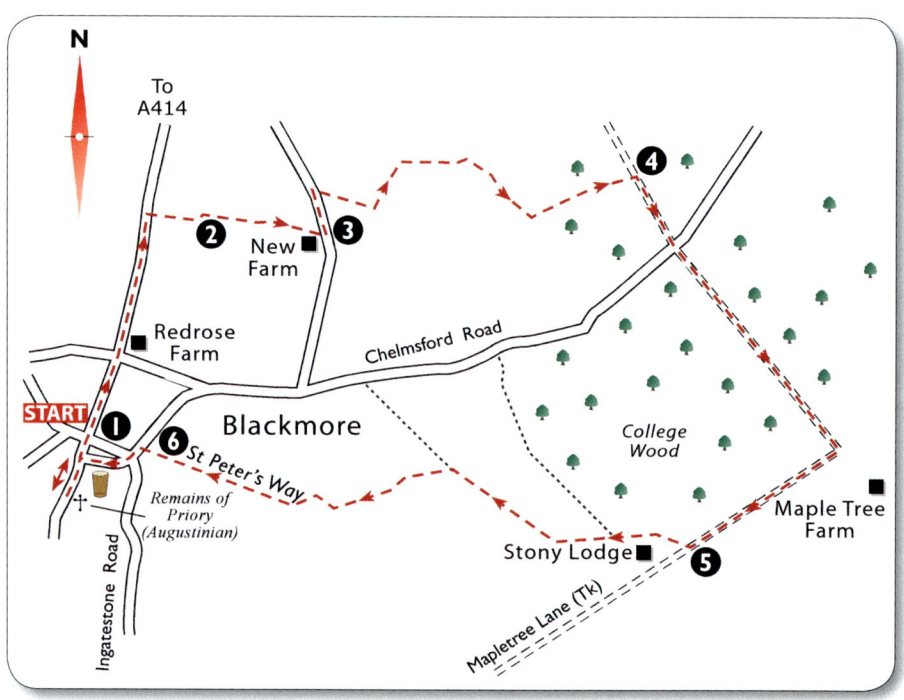

continue along the left edge of the next field. Cross a stile in a fence then turn left at a waymarker over a bridge-stile combination. At an immediate fork, go right. This woodland path through **Parsons Spring** can be difficult to see at first but widens later – if there is snow on the ground your dog will find the way! After much meandering you reach a concrete track.

4 Go right along the track, which in springtime is lined with daffodils. Prepare to reach a lane and go straight across into **Birch Spring**. Fork right at the start and follow a track, which is almost straight through this beautiful deciduous wood. Eventually reach a path junction by an old gatepost and waymarker with blue arrows. Turn right here to walk just inside the wood edge. The track is lined by ancient field boundaries – banks so old that they are surmounted by mature trees. The track dwindles and arrives at a lane.

5 Turn right and walk to the right of wooden gates to **Stony Lodge**. Walk along the surfaced drive, passing an elegant pond and stylish house on the left, and keep forward to join a track that follows the right edge of a huge field. The red disc on the waymarker denotes St Peter's Way, a 41-mile footpath from Chipping Ongar to the Dengie Peninsular. Keep forward when the track swings sharply right and at a waymarker with multiple arrows, go left across the field to trees, which surround a fishing lake. Keep to the left of the lake and continue to a gap in the hedge ahead. Once through go half right to cut a corner and rejoin the right edge of the field. Just past the field corner, go through a barrier and walk straight across the next field to a road.

6 Cross and go left. Turn right to pass between duck ponds then veer left across the green to pick up a drive and turn right. You will pass Jericho Cottage, which houses an antique shop and tea rooms. Continue to **Church Street** and turn left. At the end, **Jericho Priory** is to the left and the **Priory church** is ahead. Retrace your steps and continue to the crossroads with its pubs and excellent examples of pargeting to the right. Keep forward to return to your car.

Enjoying the scents of the woodland.

11

Chafford Gorges

Warren Gorge.

It is difficult to decide what is most remarkable about the Chafford Gorges – the astonishing variety of plant and insect life or the fact that this attractive landscape is in the midst of a highly built-up area. Certainly few Essex walkers, unless they live locally, will have had any contact with this magnificent nature reserve run by the Essex Wildlife Trust. Originally an upland chalk area, a large proportion of Chafford Hundred was quarried from the 18th century until 1960. Many of the derelict quarries were redeveloped for housing, leaving this oasis of three gorges for us to enjoy.

Paths are lined with bushes and trees and frequent clearings support a mass of chalk-loving plants, especially attractive in late springtime when nine species of orchid can be identified. The backdrop to all these delights are the chalk cliffs rising from the lakes, which, although originally gravel pits, now seem to totally complement this rich scenic treat.

Barney, a 2-year-old Lakeland terrier cross, had a great time on this walk – he particularly liked the flights of steps, which he managed quite easily, and he relished the chance of a dip in each of the three lakes.

Terrain

The paths are often good; some are chalky and can be slippery if wet – especially the steep descent at the end of stage 1. Steps are installed at most of the steep sections.

Where to park

The free car park (NB: closes at 5pm). (GR TQ600794) **Postcode:** RM16 6RW. Note that Sat Navs can lead you astray just before the car park. **OS map:** Explorer 162 Greenwich & Gravesend.

How to get there

Leave the A1306 on the A1012, following signs to Chafford Hundred. At the first roundabout, turn right into Devonshire Road. Take the next right into Drake Road, following a brown sign to Chafford Gorges until you see the sign for the car park.

Nearest refreshments

Back along Drake Road, (**Postcode:** RM16 6PP) is the Sandmartin pub which boasts a good selection of beers and a standard Green King menu. (☎ 01375 481056).

The Walk

· ·

❶ Return to the main part of **Drake Road**, cross over and turn left. Go right at **Merlin Close** and, after a few yards, take a path through the hedge on the left to turn immediately right through a kissing gate. Stay with this path, eventually swinging to the right with views of the oil storage at **Tank Farm**. At a T-junction of paths, go left, steeply downhill to a road.

❷ Go left. Just after the welcome to **Chafford Hundred** sign, cross the road to the right and go through a kissing gate up a raised path. As you approach the

Dog factors

· ·

Distance: 5 miles / 8 km.
Road walking: Surprisingly little, considering the location – 600m.
Livestock: None, except ducks on the lakes and numerous other dogs.
Stiles: None.
Nearest vets: Medivet, Chafford Hundred.

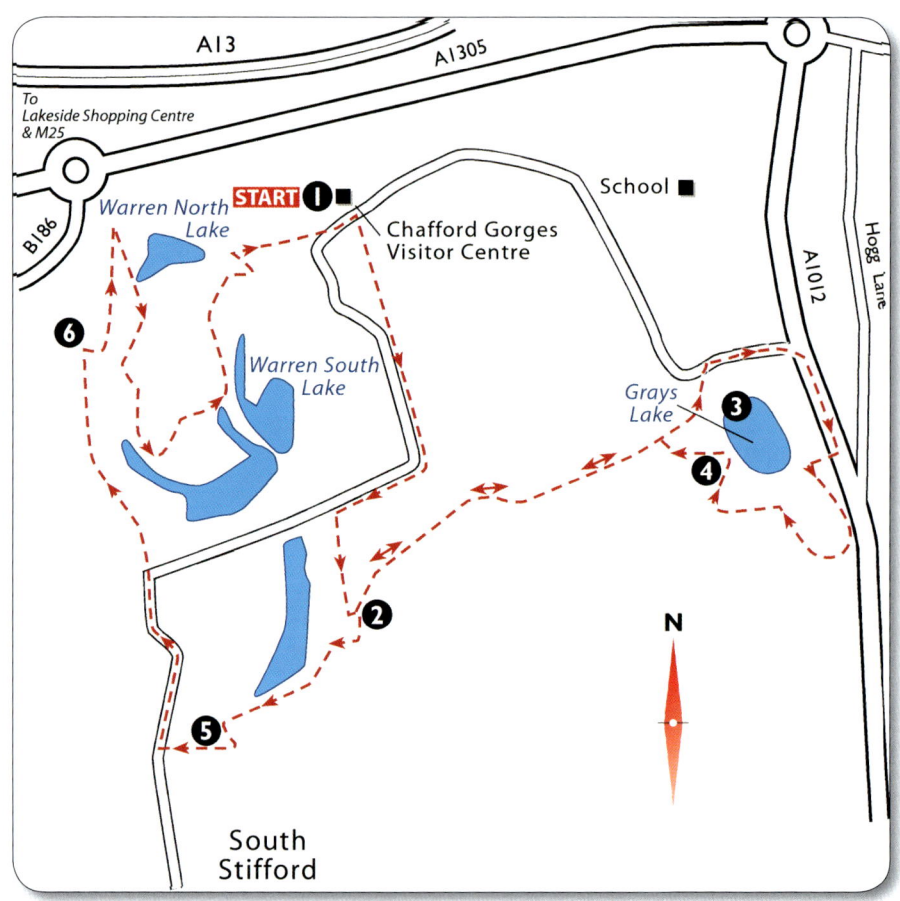

cliffs, you will come to some concrete standing; keep forward on the well-defined path ahead, which soon has a wooden fence on the left. Continue on this main path, ignoring a path on the right, soon with a fence on the right, as you gradually climb to an open metal gate.

3 The path ahead is closed but, if you wish, you can proceed about 100m to view a selection of **Sarson Stones** scattered on the right before reaching a permanent barrier. Return to the gate to continue the walk. Before the gate, descend left to go right along a pavement which you follow right past a roundabout. Go right through a kissing gate by a lamppost and cross to some steps down to a path. Turn left. A little later, at the start of a clearing, go hard right down a flight of steep steps. When faced with a choice at the bottom, go right across a bridge and up a few more steps into more mature woodland. (You should now notice signs of an old railway in the form of rails and sleepers). At the end of a clearing, at a T-junction, go right. Just after another clearing there is a narrow path going forward – ignore this and swing left with the main track. On your right is **Grays Lake**, which you will have viewed from above.

4 Swing left with the path then, on passing a bench, go to the right corner and eventually up some roped steps. Go left on a cross-track and retrace your steps back to the road. Cross and go left. Go past the exit from the steep path you used earlier and turn right at a junction. (It's worth going down the steps ahead to look at **Lion Gorge Lake** – you cannot continue far around as the path is reserved for fishers.) Turn left along a broad track below the cliff, passing a small car park and continuing through a kissing gate to soon go left to zigzag up to a road.

5 Go right. Turn right into **Lancaster Road** and immediately cross via the bollards on the left to a cycle track. Go right; you should now be walking along a pavement with the cycle track to your right, separated from the road by a bank. At a roundabout, cross and go left past the children's play area. Keep to the walkway when the road swings left and continue, crossing drives, eventually reaching a junction with a cycle track marked out.

6 Go right, keeping to the walkers' pavement. Reach an interpretation board and go right through a kissing gate down a rough-surfaced path. Ignore an

early path to the left, pass between two lakes and go right. Fork right at the next junction, keeping near to the water's edge go to the right of a gated compound. When you reach the edge of the lake's boundary, swing left at a bench. At the next junction by a picnic area go right to zigzag your way up to what was the Visitor Centre. Turn right at the top then left to reach the car park.

Lion Gorge Lake.

Terling and the Essex Way

Dogs find the ford particularly appealing for a dip.

There are many wide field verges on this walk where the well-behaved dog can be let off the lead to scamper up and down beside the cropped fields. Barney, a 2-year-old Lakeland terrier cross, managed this walk on a very hot day with aplomb.

Terling village has some extremely attractive houses of varying architectural styles and periods. The church at Fairstead is an early attraction as it is approached up a very gentle slope and is well worth a visit. Towards the end you can detour to look at the smock mill and eventually cross a ford – although you would be well advised to use the bridge provided.

Dog factors

Distance: 5¼ miles / 8.4 km.

Road walking: About ¾ mile but the majority of this is along extremely quiet country lanes.

Livestock: The farming in this area is predominantly arable but you may encounter game birds.

Stiles: None.

Nearest vets: Spring Lodge Veterinary Hospital, Witham.

Terrain

Much of this walk is along the Essex Way on good paths and cleared field edges. The farming is arable and there is some woodland. All gradients are gentle.

Where to park

Alongside Terling village hall where there is plenty of free parking (GR TL770150). **Postcode:** CM3 2PS. **OS map:** Explorer 183 Chelmsford & The Rodings.

How to get there

Turn off the A12, which runs between Chelmsford and Colchester, on the B1137 to Hatfield Peverel. Take a turning north, over the A12, past the station, to Terling. Reach a triangular green with the village sign and go straight across on a private road to the village hall.

Nearest refreshments

The Square and Compasses pub in Fuller Street, just round the corner near the start of point 4, is a truly excellent pub, which welcomes dogs in the bar area. The food is of a really high standard with all the usual pub favourites plus interesting specials. At least three real ales are available, all on gravity. ☎ 01245 361477. www.thesquareandcompasses.co.uk. If you would prefer something near the end of the walk, the Owl's Hill Tearoom which is open from 9.30 to 3.30 and doubles as GP surgery might fit the bill. Opposite is the Rayleigh Arms which serves traditional pub food.

The Walk

1 Walk back to the main road and turn left. Just past the end of the houses and nearly opposite a road junction, turn right alongside **Monk's Cottage**. Keep forward past a barrier, as the drive becomes a track and continues to the left of a hedge.

Essex – A Dog Walker's Guide

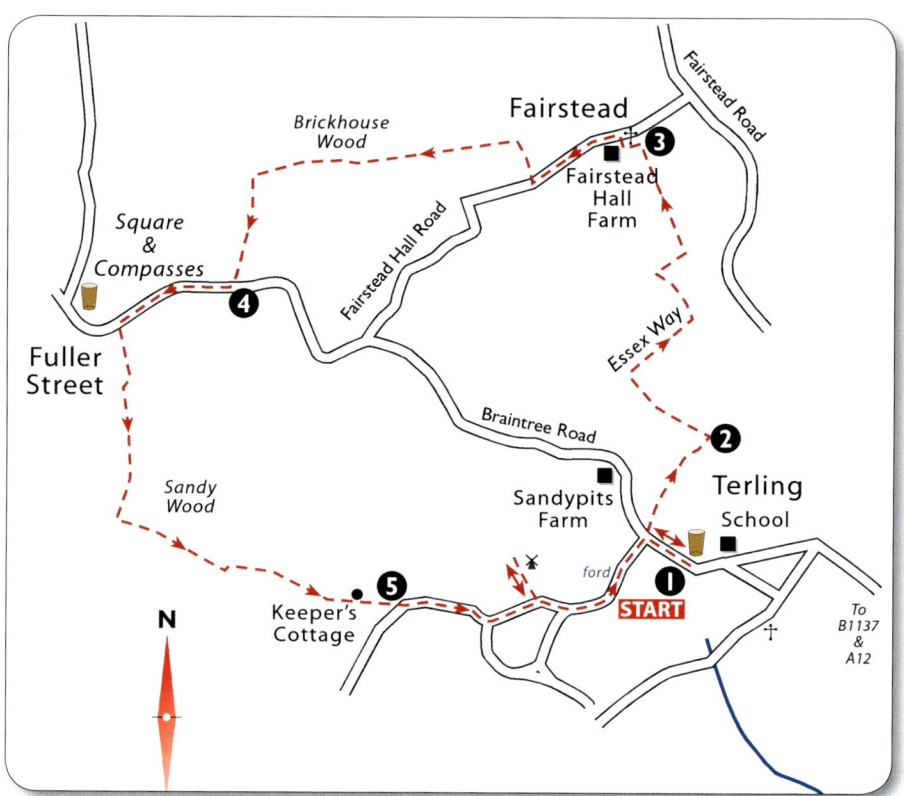

2 At the field boundary go left with the **Essex Way**, still with a hedge to the right. At the end of this field, swing right and then left to go right of a waymarker along the lower edge of the next field. Soon you are between a young plantation on the left and mature trees to the right. Turn left at a waymarker showing the Essex Way poppies symbol to enter woodland. Follow the main path as it travels the short distance through the wood (it can be eerie here at dusk). Emerge at a field edge and go right. The track swings left at a marker. You are now heading towards **Fairstead church**. Descend to a bridge and walk straight up the field to join a hedged path. Cross a bridge and go left through a graveyard. Go left again to enter the churchyard and go clockwise around the church to the road. The church, which is mainly Norman but built with Roman bricks, is well worth a visit with its small organ and remnants of medieval paintings of the Passion.

3 Turn left. Pass **Fairstead Hall** on the left and ignore the first footpath sign up a concrete lane to the right. Keep forward up a gentle hill. Take a field edge path on the right at a concrete fingerpost. At the boundary, turn left with the path so that you still have the hedge to your right. At the end of the field, keep forward to the right of the wood then pass under a pylon to continue to the left of **Brickhouse Wood**. Cross a bridge at the end of the field and immediately turn left to walk, with the hedge left, alongside two fields to a road.

4 Turn right. Continue past the sign for **Fuller Street** and as the road is starting to swing right, just after a small speed limit sign and before a house, turn left past a barrier. (If you want to visit the **Square and Compasses**, continue along the road for 200m to a junction – the pub is on the right.) Keep forward, crossing to the right of the hedge by a waymarker. Go right at the end of the field and soon left to cross a bridge over a stream. Keep forward under power lines to the right of **Sandy Wood**, which is massed with bluebells in the spring. Follow the wood edge around to the left, joining a farm track and keeping forward at the boundary on a wide grassy field margin. Where the wood ends, swing left for a few yards then go right on a clear cross-field path and up the right fenced edge of a narrow field. The track becomes a surfaced drive at **Keeper's Cottage** and takes you to a road.

5 Turn left. Keep to this road, ignoring side turnings, until you reach **Hull Lane** where you turn left. A little later, turn left on **Mill Lane** to inspect the mill. This is an example of a smock mill. Built at the start of the 19th century it has lost its main sails but retains the fantail, which turned the top of the mill into the wind. In 1950 the last miller was trapped in the machinery and died. Return

to the road and continue left at the junction to a ford. (Despite the warning notices, motorists frequently take a chance at this deceptively deep ford and have to be pulled out by the fire brigade – Barney thought that it was ideal for a cooling dip.) Continue to the road and turn right. Retrace your steps to the green and turn right to your car.

Fairstead church

Colne Engaine

Good paths through delightful woodland are a feature of this walk.

The name of the village of Colne Engaine derives from its link with the River Colne and the fact that the family of Engaines were the main 13th-century landlords. The walk, which leaves the village for another, Pebmarsh, travels along both sides of the valley of a stream locally known as the Peb. Both villages were heavily engaged in the textiles industry in the past but now they are quiet dormitories. Not only are they attractive and serene but they both feature Tudor churches with beautiful porches.

The real stars of the route, however, are the many stretches of woodland where, depending on the season, you will see wild garlic, bluebells and campion, along with a whole variety of other wild flowers. Here you may also encounter deer and observe the results of badgers' energetic excavations. For dogs the woods are a source of odours that require almost constant attention.

Terrain

A walk best undertaken in spring or early summer to catch the flower displays. The paths across arable fields are promptly and generously reinstated so that there is little difficulty in following the route. Whilst undulating, there are no arduous climbs. Near the aptly-named Pebmarsh there are parts of the walk that are damp underfoot all year round.

Where to park

In the free car park next to Colne Engaine church (GR TL850303). **Postcode:** C06 2EX. **OS map:** Explorer 195 Braintree & Saffron Walden.

How to get there

Colne Engaine is best reached by a turning north off the A1124, which runs between Halstead and the A12 west of Colchester.

Nearest refreshments

There are two pubs passed on this walk, the Kings Head (☎ 01787 267942) which is roughly halfway round at Pebmarsh, and the Five Bells (☎ 01787 224166) near the end. Both are dog friendly with water bowls and treats and they both serve real ales along with simple bar menus as well as more substantial meals.

The Walk

① From the car park go right immediately, passing the church and going left on a paved path and out through a lychgate. Turn right, then left along **Church Street**. Go straight across the green by the village sign to find a path

Dog factors

Distance: 6 miles / 9.6 km.
Road walking: Approximately 1 mile of quiet lanes – the majority during stage 2.
Livestock: Your only encounter with farm livestock will be during stage 5 when there may be cattle in the field.
Stiles: 3 – these are open stiles that were no problem for Sam, a 12-year-old St Bernard cross. A gate at the start of stage 5 might prove difficult for an extra long dog but there is another gate to the left that can be used as an alternative.
Nearest vets: The Forge Veterinary Centre, Halstead.

with overhanging trees, which emerges on the right-hand edge of a field. Follow a track down to a road.

2 Turn left. Follow the road past Brickhouse Farm then head uphill. Around 20m after passing **Nightingale Cottages**, go right on a fenced path. Continue diagonally right across a field to a bridge and along a hedged path. Descend on a track through a strip of woodland. The track swings to the right to join a cross-track; go left to follow this track up between trees and bushes. At the top, at a major junction of tracks, go right through a grassy gap. Go left along the field-edge and take a track going diagonally right across the field. Go forward at the end over a bridge and immediately turn left to keep to the left of a rather boggy slice of woodland to reach a lane.

3 Go right on **Water Lane**. Ignore the entrance to a housing estate on the right and continue to a junction opposite the **Kings Head**. Turn right past the **Pebmarsh** village sign and right again at **Mill Lane** opposite the church. After 200m fork left off the lane on a track, passing a thatched house with

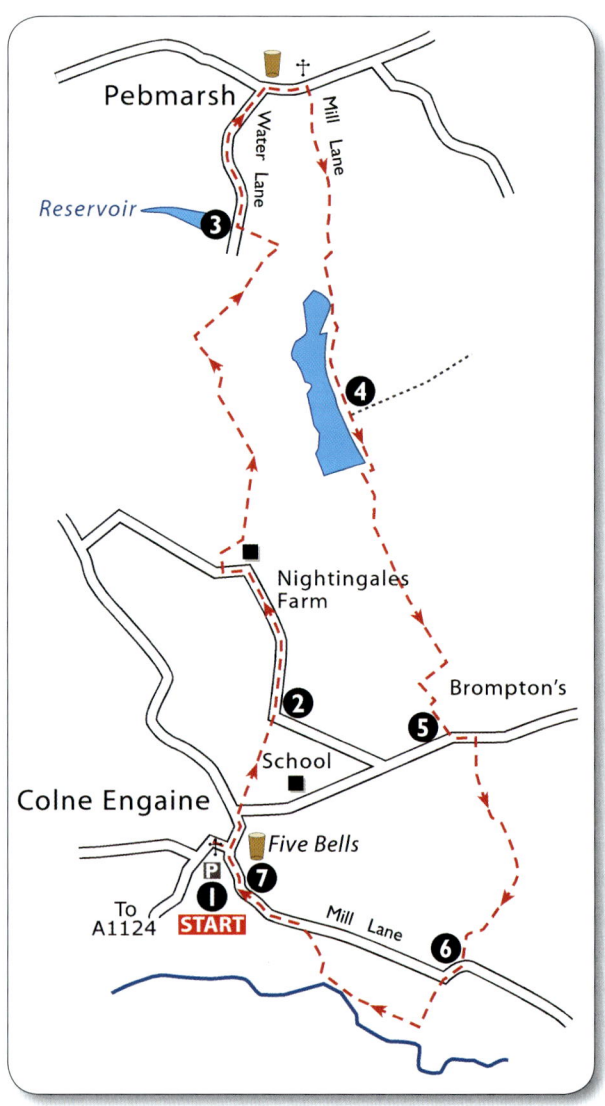

a prominent garage. Enter woodland. Keep forward at a post bearing multiple waymarks. This delightful path, showing signs of badger activity, soon descends to the lower edge of the wood then joins a fenced section to enter more woodland. Once across the bridge you should be able to glimpse the reservoir to your right. After another fenced section you will join the right edge of a field.

4 Keep forward on a broad track alongside the water until you reach the dam where you go right for 10m and then left along the edge of woodland. Cross a bridge into the next field and continue along the right edge, ignoring a footpath to the right, to eventually enter the wood. Emerge from the wood to continue on the right-hand field edge, ignoring paths to right and left.

Bluebells carpet the woods in springtime.

In the next, narrower field, ignore the ford to the right and go forward and right before a gate. Cross a bridge to follow a fenced path around a willow plantation with a good view of Brompton's, a restored private house. Reach a road.

5 Turn left and go right at a concrete fingerpost. Walk up the right-hand side of the meadow. On reaching a six-bar metal gate on the right, go left across an earth bridge and then right alongside the first line of willows, with a ditch to the right (this is the one field where you might encounter cattle). Leave the field by the far right corner over an earthen bridge – soon followed by another bridge. Continue within a fence with a mill stream to the right and alongside a pond. Cross a bridge and turn left on a track to a road.

6 Go right. On the corner, beside a cottage, go left to walk along a left field edge and continue through a strip of woodland, to turn right along the trackbed of a disused railway. At a junction, go right down the slope then swing left to pass a weir and gauging station on the **Colne**. At the field boundary, leave the river to go up a slope to a bridge on the left and immediately turn right uphill with the plantation to your left. At the top go left and continue to a corner where a right turn will bring you to a field edge. Keep forward parallel to the road, which you rejoin when it begins to swing right.

7 The **Five Bells** is on the right. Fork left by a telephone kiosk up past the church to a road. Turn left to the car park.

Sam taking a breather.

Fordstreet and the River Colne

The impressive Chappel viaduct.

The valley of the River Colne provides some of the best walking in Essex. The river is rarely more attractive than when it passes through the borders of Aldham and Fordstreet at the start of this walk. The route then continues along a section of the Essex Way before turning off towards Chappel. Here the dominant feature is the viaduct; built in just two years and finished in 1849 it is a tribute to the pride that the Victorians took in their workmanship. Its 32-arched structure comprises 4.5 million bricks and supports part of the single-track railway running between Marks Tey and Sudbury.

Our companion, George, a 4-year-old brown Labrador, thoroughly enjoyed this walk, mainly because there were long stretches where he could run freely off the lead.

Terrain

This is an easy, quiet walk although there are some stretches during stage 5 which become muddy after heavy rain.

Where to park

Walkers who are going to visit the café at the Shoulder of Mutton (GR TL920272) before or after their walk are welcome to use the car park but they should let the owners know first. **Postcode:** CO6 3LL. **OS Map:** Two maps cover this walk: Explorer 184 Colchester Harwich & Clacton-on-Sea and 195 Braintree & Saffron Walden Halstead & Great Dunmow.

How to get there

The Shoulder of Mutton is on the A1124, which runs between Halstead and Colchester, beside a bridge over the River Colne on the border of Ford street and Aldham.

Nearest refreshments

The Shoulder of Mutton is an antiques centre with an upmarket café which is open every day, serving breakfast up to 11.30 am and sandwiches, baguettes and light bites until 3 pm. ☎ 01206 687287.

For a more substantial meal, you may wish to stop at the Swan Inn (☎ 01787 222 353) which is very near the start of stage 4 of this walk. www.swaninn-chappel.com

Dog factors

· ·

Distance: 4½ miles / 7.2 km.
Road walking: Approximately 600m along a pavement out of Chappel (point 4).
Livestock: There are a couple of fields in point 2 where you may encounter sheep and cattle.
Stiles: 1 – and this is redundant.
Nearest vets: Ark Veterinary Centre, Lexden.

The Walk

• •

1 Cross the main road and turn left over the bridge. Immediately after a drive to **Bridge House** turn right along a narrow path between a wall and fence. Keep forward, crossing a bridge, to arrive alongside the **River Colne**. Continue, passing various enterprises of the garden centre on the left to go between a pillbox and a concrete landing stage.

2 Enter a field with a stand of conifers on the left. Keep forward onto a track on the right edge of two large fields. Eventually this track rejoins the edge

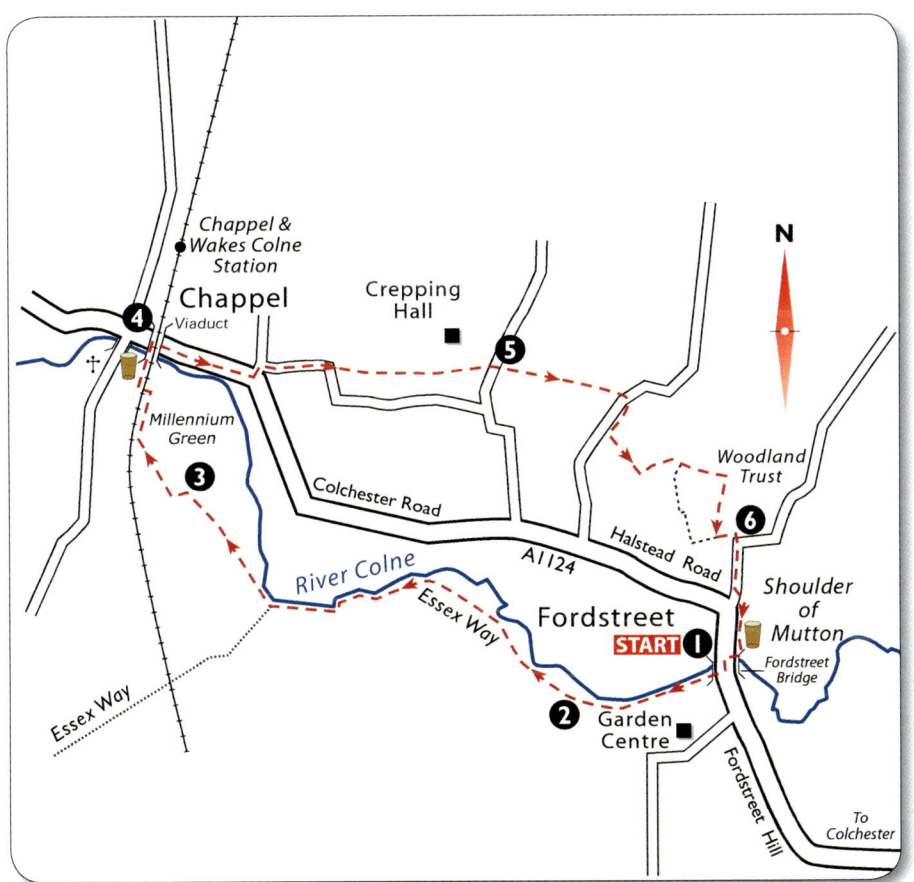

On the way to the viaduct.

of the Colne; it enters a second, smaller field, which you leave by a bridge in a corner. Keep along the right edge of the following pasture. Ignore an attractive brick bridge on the right and go through a gate by a pillbox. Keep forward in the next field through a kissing-gate. In the following field continue alongside the hedge. When this ends, go straight ahead across the field to a margin marked by a ditch. Now go diagonally left to join a fence, which you follow right to a fingerpost.

3 Turn left to join a lane. After about 30m turn right up a slope by a waymarker. Go diagonally left across the field to a bridge in the corner and turn right. You are now walking parallel with a railway line, which is later carried by the viaduct that you will have noticed earlier. Soon you will pass the **Millennium Green** on the right, alongside the viaduct. (If you feel like a sandwich whilst watching your dog run about, the green with its picnic tables could be just the place.) Look through the centre of the viaduct to really appreciate the art of the Victorian bricklayers. Keep forward alongside the viaduct. The path eventually swings left and you cross a bridge on the right to reach a road.

④ Go right under the viaduct. After less than ¼ mile, at the top of the rise, go left at the junction and then right along **Vernons Road**. Just after a sharp right-hand corner, turn left through a gate to walk along the right field edge to a waymarker at the corner. Cross a bridge and walk up through a strip of woodland. Continue uphill to the left of an area of bushes and trees, aiming to the right of trees ahead. Walk along a line of conifers to the left and, towards the top of the hill, fork left and go through a gate. Go forward, initially alongside a fence, with **Crepping Hall** to the left, to a gate ahead. Reach a lane.

⑤ Cross to join a path on a right-hand field edge, which feeds into a hedged path past houses to a drive and then a lane. Go right and join the right edge of a field at a fingerpost. Follow the hedge round to the left and continue with it on the far side, past a track with green markers to go right over a bridge. Climb straight up a path (ignoring a waymarker to steps on the right). Enter a field and go forward along the right edge of the field. Continue alongside trees, eventually, at a junction, following them right down the hill. At the bottom of the field go left, soon going down steps on the right to a drive.

⑥ Cross over the lane and go right on a parallel fenced path. Keep forward, ignoring metal kissing gates to the left and other paths. Reach a substantial Woodland Trust information board and go right over a bridge to the **Shoulder of Mutton**.

The attractive bridge at point 3 of the walk.

Birch and the Roman River

Approaching a lodge at Birch Park.

Few would dispute that Colchester is one of the most important sites of the Roman occupation in Britain and this walk takes us to Gosbecks Archaeological Park where, carefully etched on the ground, the outlines of two important buildings dating back to AD 100 can be seen. Interpretation boards enable us to envisage the original structures, a theatre and temple, and the astonishing sophistication of the architects.

Starting from an isolated road junction we pass through Birch Park before gradually descending into the valley of the Roman River, which is characterised by pleasant, lush woodland. After emerging on the plains surrounding Colchester to visit the Roman sites we return, once again, along the valley. Barney really enjoyed this walk – there were plenty of opportunities to run and sniff with the bonus of two dips in the Roman River – but he didn't seem to be much interested in the Roman sites!

Terrain

Most of the walk is along good paths and solid farm tracks. There are a couple of places in the river valley that can become very muddy after rain. Gradients are gentle.

Where to park

There is a small area of waste ground on a junction of the B1022 about halfway between Birch and Heckfordbridge and almost opposite a park lodge with a bus shelter on one side and a bench in the middle of a tiny green. (GR TL942208). **Postcode:** CO2 0LU. **OS map:** Explorer 184 Colchester.

How to get there

The road junction where we park is on the B1022, roughly halfway between Tiptree and Colchester and approximately ½ mile north of Birch.

Nearest refreshments

There are no refreshment stops on the walk. The Hare and Hounds at Birch Green (CO2 0PN) is about a mile south. It is a very popular pub and dogs are welcomed with enthusiasm in the bar – if you intend to eat, you should book as tables there are limited. ☎ 01206 330459. www.thehareandhound.co.uk

The Walk

. . . .

1 Start the walk by crossing the road and going down a wide track to the right of **Birch Park Lodge**, keeping forward between fenced fields. Over to the right

Dog factors

. . . .

Distance: 5½ miles / 8.8 km.
Road walking: ½ mile.
Livestock: None.
Stiles: None.
Nearest vets: Medivet, Maldon Road.

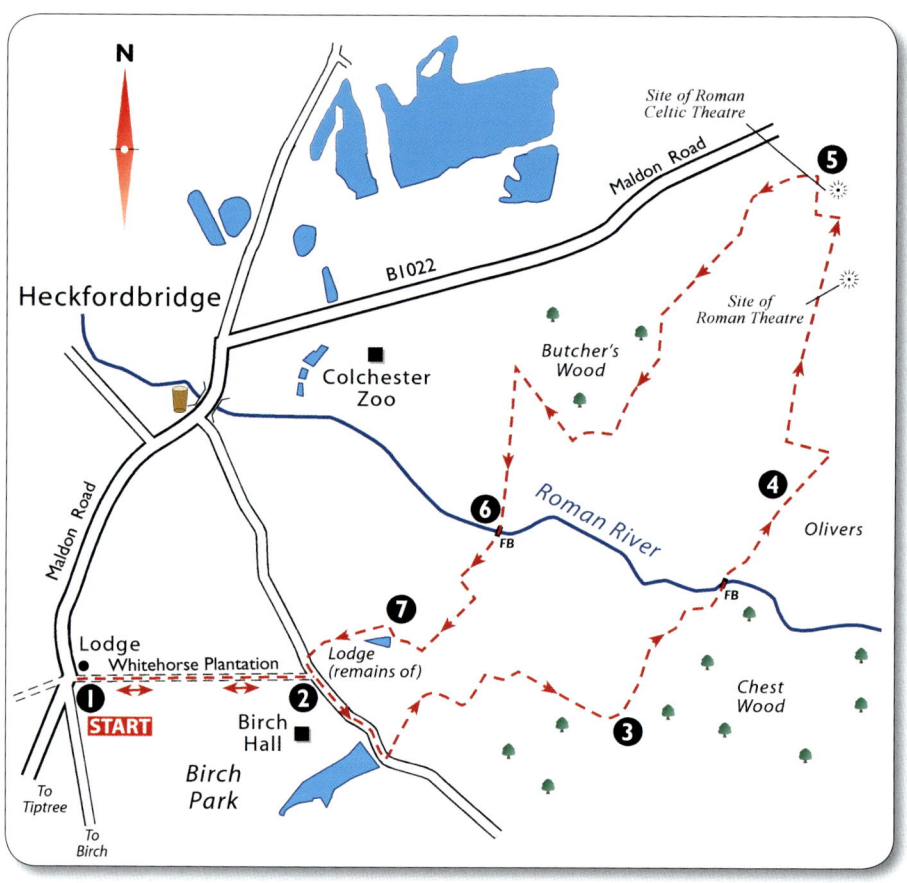

you gradually get a splendid view of **Birch Hall**. Reach a road by a second lodge.

② Go right. At the end of a lake on the right, go left on another broad track. Keep to this main track as it swings left and, on approaching the buildings of **Hill Farm**, fork right. Go right again at the next fork. Eventually you arrive at a waymarked junction.

③ Go left on a semi-surfaced path to descend gently through trees to a footbridge over the **Roman River** and nature reserve. Continue straight uphill to a major junction of paths at **Olivers**.

4 Keep forward, with buildings to your right, to join a lane. After about 100m go left at a fingerpost and along the right edge of a field. Keep with this edge, swinging right, until you reach a pair of paths on the right – one of which is a bridleway. Take the one on the left-hand side and immediately turn left to keep your previous direction, now walking alongside the Roman site. (The first interpretation board over to the right explains the outline of the **Roman Theatre** on the ground, together with an illustration of what it originally looked like.) At the field boundary go left (now on your right is the site of a **Romano-Celtic Temple** with an interpretation board in the distance). Follow the field hedge as it goes left, then up to twin oak trees to the field corner.

5 Go left across the boundary to a bridleway, then right to walk with the hedge on your right. Later the path does a definite left turn with a wooded valley to your right. At the far end of the field, reach a cross-track with four tall tree stumps to the left. Go right on a farm track downhill to cross a stream by an earth bridge and climb again. At the top of the rise, with a view of a ruined church on the outskirts of **Colchester Zoo** ahead, turn a very sharp left downhill. Keep forward at the bottom to a footbridge.

6 Re-cross the **Roman River**. Follow the waymarked path through beautiful woodland. Climb steadily, looking for a willow plantation on the right. Follow the avenue of trees. At the end, go right uphill, then left to overlook a lake below. Reach a fence and then a track.

7 Turn left, past a house, to join a drive and reach a road. Go left, then right before the lodge to retrace your steps to your car.

Purleigh

A lush green path.

Purleigh is a quiet village surrounding its church, which is perched on a hill. The village sign, depicting the now rare bittern, alludes to the Anglo-Saxon meaning of the village name. Purleigh's history is of a once-bustling village, which reached its heyday in the 16th and 17th centuries when trades and alehouses proliferated.

This walk provides a straightforward exploration of the village's surrounds. Fields with long-grass borders and stretches of scrub provide ample areas for free running and investigation by the curious dog. The route takes you to one of the few now recognisable remains of a First World War airfield, where fighters were launched to attack German Gotha bombers and Zeppelins. Whilst most of the walk provides extensive views, these are enhanced towards the end when it climbs to the church. At the entrance to the church is a hibiscus that was reared in George Washington's garden in Vermont. George's great grandfather was rector of St Margaret's church in the 17th century.

Terrain

The walk is mainly along field edges, with some quiet lanes. The ground in point 3 is uneven and, although it will not inconvenience your dog unless it is very small, the walker is advised to wear boots with ankle support. Most paths remain relatively dry even after heavy rain.

Where to park

In the free playing field car park to the south of the village. It is best to arrive after 11 am when the local dog walkers have left. (GR TL 837019). **Postcode:** CM3 6PX. **OS map:** Explorer 183 Chelmsford & The Rodings.

How to get there

Leave the A12 Colchester to London road on the A414 towards Maldon. Purleigh is signed off the B1010, which runs between Burnham-on-Crouch and the A414 east of Danbury. The car park is at the southern end of the village on the road to Cold Norton.

Nearest refreshments

The Purleigh Bell, a 16th-century pub, can be visited during stage 6 of the walk. It is a comfortable place and welcomes dogs. A good range of real ales is available along with an interesting menu as well as the usual pub fare of pies and snacks. The garden offers views over to Maldon and the surrounding area. Closed Mondays and Tuesdays. ☎ 01621 828348. www.purleighbell.co.uk

The Walk

● ●

1 Leave the parking area and continue along the hedge to exit the playing field by a gap in the corner to a road. Keep forward along the right-hand side of the road. Just before the de-restriction sign, turn right at a fingerpost through a metal gate. Go up a fenced path and continue on the right field edge. Cross a bridge and continue with the hedge to the left. Reach **Hackmans Lane**.

Dog factors

● ●

Distance: 4¼ miles / 6.8 km.
Road walking: 1 mile, mostly along quiet lanes.
Livestock: None but you may meet horse riders.
Stiles: 1.
Nearest vets: Edgewood, Purleigh surgery.

2 Cross and turn left. Pass three drives, including one to **Little Whitmans Farm** to reach a fingerpost on the right. After about 5m fork right, going diagonally right across the field to go through a gate and cross a low barrier. Swing left and go forward to walk up the right edge of a field. Continue in the next field to the left of the hedge then, at a corner, cross a bridge to go straight across the field. Reach a gate but do not go through it. (Over to your left are the huts and water tower of a First World War airfield where there is now a museum – you could follow the footpath through the gate if you wanted to extend your walk; Stow Maries Great War Aerodrome).

3 Turn right. Keep forward with the hedge on the left to cross bridges into the next and following field. Once over a third field and bridge you reach a concrete drive and turn right to reach the road.

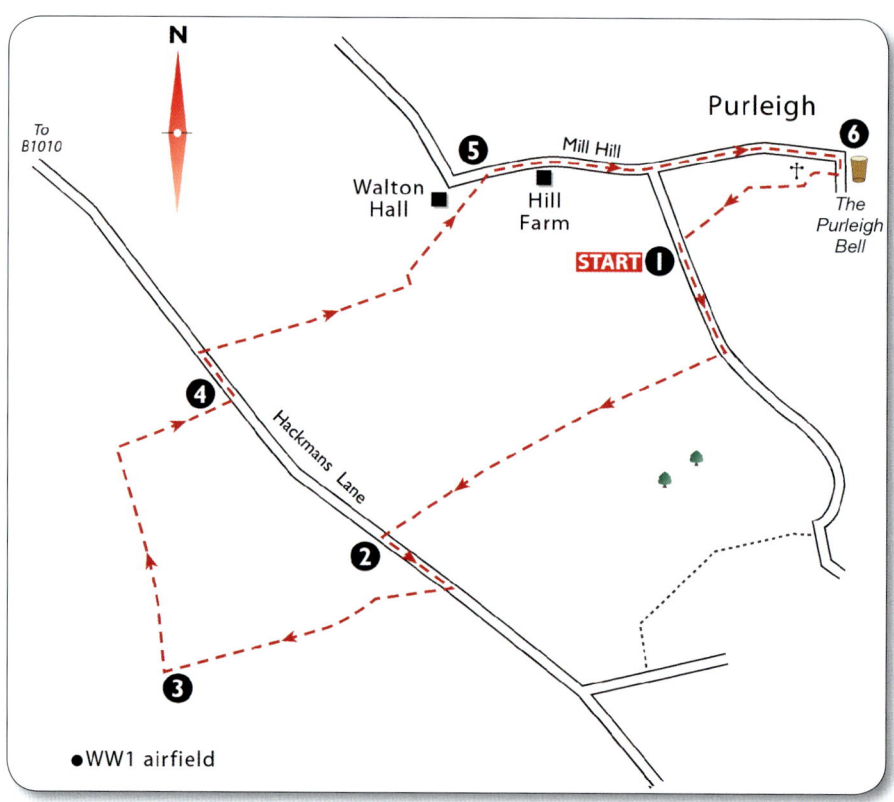

The Bell inn near the end of the route.

4 Cross and go left. Turn right at the next fingerpost to walk along the left edge of the field following a ditch. At the brow of the field, follow the ditch to the left. If the farmer has reinstated the path go diagonally right across the field, otherwise at the next boundary, go right before an open barn alongside some conifers and follow the hedge as it meanders around the field until you reach a corner gap to emerge on **Mill Hill**.

5 Turn right and keep forward past the village hall along **The Glebe**. Continue past the community shop and village sign to climb the hill to the church. (The churchyard, on the left, provides extensive views of **Osea Island** and **Maldon**.)

6 Go right into the church grounds. (The shrub you pass just before the main entrance is the hibiscus that came from George Washington's garden in Vermont.) Reach a gate. To visit the **Purleigh Bell** pub, go through and swing left – otherwise go right along the wall then left along a fenced path. Go right over a stile and down the right edge of a field. A bridge returns you to the playing field where you will see your car in the distance.

Paglesham

The sea wall.

This is one of two walks in this book that explore the semi wilderness of the estuaries for which Essex is famous and about which many authors have eulogised. Most of your time you will be gazing across Paglesham Pool to Wallasea Island, a large and developing RSPB reserve, and later across Paglesham Creek to Burnham-on-Crouch. Birdlife is prolific here and, as with all walks of this kind, you have the benefit of a full complement of birds associated with farmland, especially kestrels, and, at certain times of the year, an abundance of sea birds – and all safe from the interference of your dog. Paglesham itself is in fact two small settlements separated by nearly three miles of roads. Both are delightful, featuring white, wooden buildings that dazzle in low sunlight.

We did this walk in very wet weather with Sam, a 12-year-old St Bernard cross, and Pip, a rescue dog of indeterminate parentage. Both intimated that they would have liked less rain but did quietly enjoy the views from the sea wall.

Terrain

This is excellent walking for both partners; the walker has the benefit of an elevated view over good paths most of the way whilst the dog will have a wonderful time up and down the banks if he/she is feeling energetic. This is likely to be quite a windy walk and you will need plenty of warm clothes in the wintertime.

Where to park

The parking place at the end of East Hall Road, Paglesham East End is small with room for five or six cars but it avoids parking near the two pubs, which can be very difficult, especially at weekends. Park leaving access to the gates (GR TQ944927). **Postcode:** SS4 2EF. Follow directions below, rather than relying on satnav to find the parking spot. **OS map:** Explorer 176 Blackwater Estuary.

How to get there

From Rochford, go through Great Stambridge, turning right at a T-junction with an unreliable signpost. Turn right on the Paglesham road opposite the Shepherd & Dog pub. Follow the signpost to East End and Paglesham. When this road swings right, go forward down a dead end called East Hall Road, which has a post box on the right-hand side. Go straight down the road, and just past a house on the corner, by a footpath sign, there is a small parking place.

Nearest refreshments

Just after point 4 in the walk you will pass a quintessentially English country pub, the Punchbowl, which has a focus on modern British cooking. It is open Wednesday to Sunday plus Bank Holidays. Dogs are welcome in the bar. (☎ 01702 660 118).

Dog factors

Distance: 5 miles / 8 km.
Road walking: None, although some use of lanes and surfaced paths.
Livestock: Lots of birds but these are separated from the paths by water. There are signs about sheep but I have never seen any on the sea wall. Of course, if they are there, the dog will need to be on a lead.
Stiles: 3 but all can be bypassed.
Nearest vets: Rochford Vet Surgery.

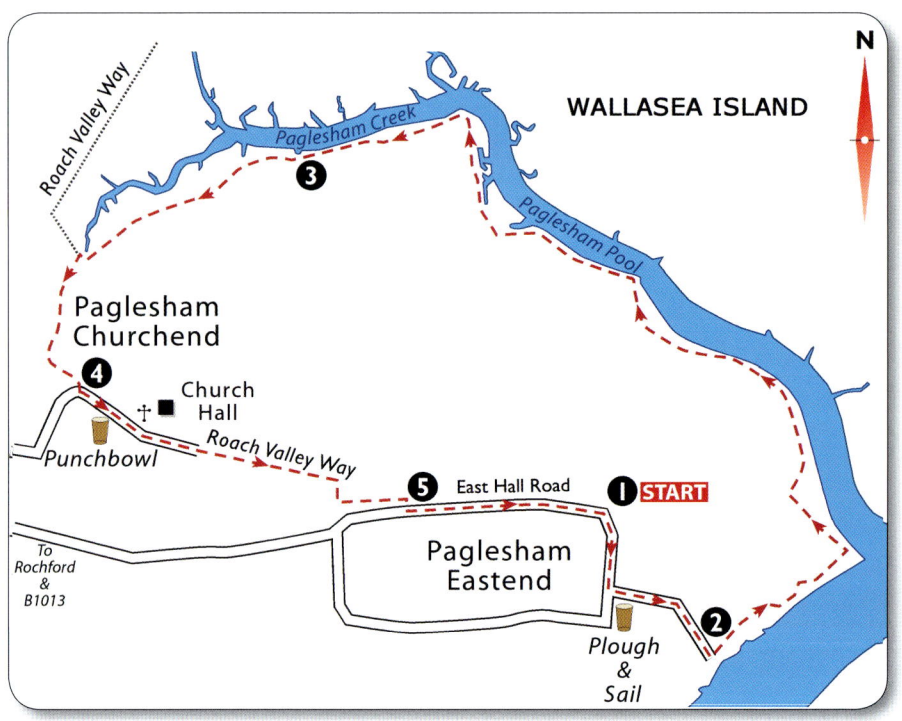

The Walk

1 Leave the parking area and go left along a short section of lane, then through a picket gate along the left-hand side of an impressive wooden-clad building. Keep to the left of the lawn to reach the right edge of a field and continue to go through another gate to join a track and go left (if you continue forward you will come to **Paglesham East End** and the **Plough & Sail pub**). Swing right with the track towards the boatyard, which you enter alongside conifers; keep forward between the boats to a slipway. Go up steps to the left.

2 Go left along the sea wall. You will now be walking along this for about 3 miles. During this time you will go through a couple of gates and to the side of three stiles. An early encounter with an information board draws your attention to the final resting place of the *Beagle*, the ship which carried Charles Darwin to South America. Your elevated position will enable you to appreciate the views across the mud flats and the salt tolerant plants to **Burnham-on-Crouch** and an off-shore wind farm on one side and the rich selection of flowering plants and patchwork of arable farmland on the other. The banked nature of the route means that whilst you casually amble along on the top, your dog can be running up and down through the long grass. Reach a second pillbox and a sluice.

3 Come down off the bank to go round the sluice then climb back up to continue your journey. Eventually, after what I hope was an enjoyable and relaxing walk, the sea wall turns sharply right to a gate and steps; don't go through the gate but do go down the steps on the left. Cross the mouth of this sluice and go ahead with a wide ditch to the right. Join a concrete path, ignore a path to the right, and continue, swinging left to eventually reach a road.

4 Pass through the village of **Paglesham Churchend** with its picturesque timber-faced pub, the **Punchbowl**, a row of houses and the church. Where the lane swings left, keep forward to the right of **Church Hall Farm** on a drive with a lake to the right. Go left of the gates to **Winton Haw** on a hedged path, continuing on a narrower path with a wooden fence. Pick up the right edge of a field and continue to follow a cross-field path to a boundary where you turn right on a surfaced drive. Swing left with the drive but leave it, ignoring a double gate to the right to pass alongside a line of barns before turning right to a lane.

5 Go left and follow the lane back to your car.

Negotiating the path through the boatyard.

Bradwell-on-Sea

The iconic St Peter's Chapel.

Although **decommissioning began** in 2002, Bradwell Power Station is still a powerful feature on the landscape for many miles around and this walk provides the opportunity to examine it at closer quarters. Before we get there we use the remnants of one of Essex's many Second World War airfields as pathways and, at one point, pass a memorial bearing the poignant reminder of the many brave lives lost in defending this country. The airfield is not the only relic of the war, though, as we also pass dozens of pillboxes.

Once on the sea wall you have the luxury of seeing unusual salt-tolerant plants, thousands of migratory birds in the autumn and views across to Mersea Island. Whilst dogs will need to be kept under control in the nature reserves of Bradwell and Cockle Spit, Barney, our Lakeland terrier cross, found plenty to interest him along the wall path and a quick dip in the sea under supervision was much appreciated. Finally, as you turn inland, you come across the Chapel of St Peter-on-the-Wall – this is probably one of the most quietly religious sites in Essex. Founded by St Cedd in AD 664, it is always open and best visited outside holiday times to really appreciate the curious stillness that pervades the unadorned building.

Terrain

This is a good walk to undertake in the winter when other outings may be muddy. Most of the walk is on good surfaces and the sea wall, whilst it may be slippery after rain, is usually mud free.

Where to park

The parking area at the end of East End Road in Bradwell, which is, in fact, a Roman road (GR TM024078). **Postcode:** CM0 7PN. **OS map:** Explorer 176 Blackwater Estuary.

How to get there

There is a complex network of roads leading to Bradwell-on-Sea, south of Maldon. The most straightforward route is to leave the Colchester to London A12 by the A414 towards Maldon. Turn onto the B1010 after Danbury and then left onto the B1018 to Latchingdon; after which you pass through the villages of Mayland, Steeple and St Lawrence. Just before reaching Bradwell-on-Sea go right at a brown sign to St Chad's, then right before a church to follow a dead-end road, East End Road. The parking area is at the end of this.

Dog factors

Distance: 6 miles / 9.5 km.
Road walking: Approximately 1 mile along roads but these tend to be deserted.
Livestock: Wild birds, especially in the autumn.
Stiles: None.
Nearest vets: Clarendon House Veterinary Centre, Maldon.

Nearest refreshments

The Kings Head on Bradwell High Street (CM0 7QN) is a large comfy pub with a couple of real ales and a range of lagers to accompany a menu which will satisfy those looking for a snack or a more substantial meal. (☎ 01621 776224).

The Walk

1 Walk back along the road you arrived by. As this is a dead-end there will be little traffic, especially during the week. You will pass a caravan site. Go under power lines and pass a road junction to a point where the road swings left.

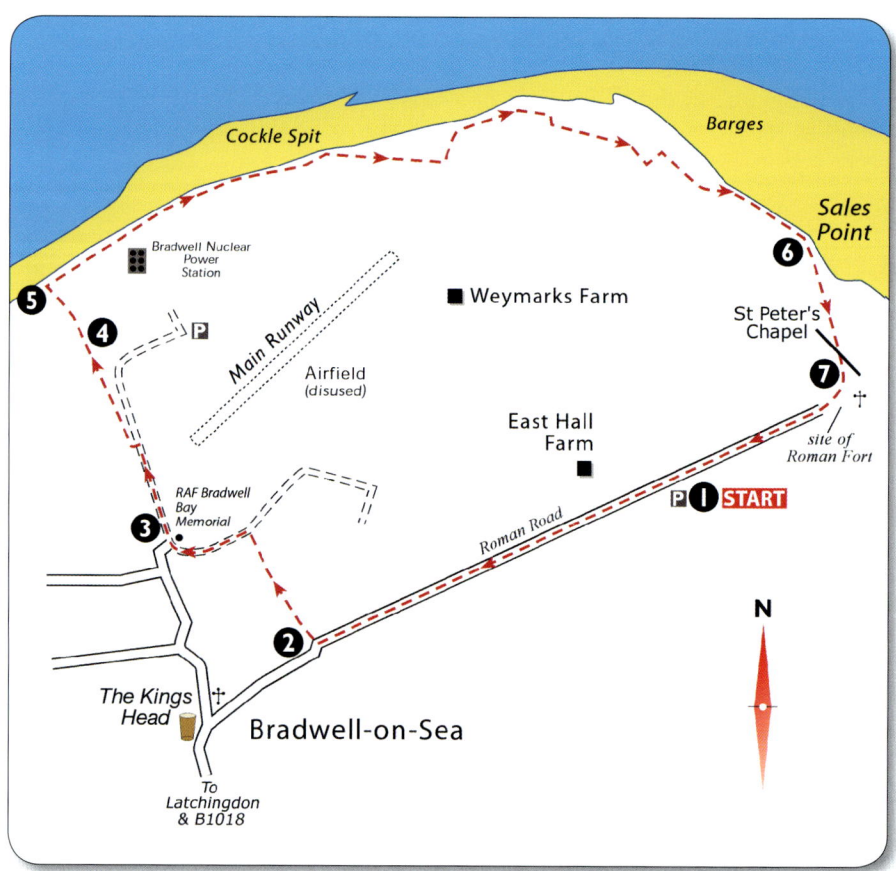

2 Turn right at a fingerpost along a concrete track. This track is one of many remnants of the Second World War airfield, **RAF Bradwell Bay**, which occupied this part of the peninsular. Ignore a bridge to the left and keep forward to a T-junction. Go left on a disused taxiing track. Reach a memorial, which commemorates the loss of 121 airmen.

3 Go right at the junction to pass what was once the main runway on the right and continue to a lone tree which shrouds a concrete fingerpost. Turn left across a field to turn right into a hedged path which is lined with bushes and small trees. (If the weather is poor or conditions are muddy, you could keep to the road.) Continue along a track and keep forward at an early fork. Go through a metal gate.

4 Keep forward, diagonally left you will see the marina at **Bradwell Waterside**, to your right is a close-up view of **Bradwell Power Station**. Reach the sea wall and climb to the top.

5 Turn right, passing the first of several pill boxes. Explore the **Cockle Spit**, a nature reserve that includes 30 acres of shell bank and extensive mudflats. It was established to help shore-nesting birds, especially the little tern. A rare British breeding sea bird, the little tern suffers from 'people pressure' on shingle beaches where it nests. After approximately 2 miles you will pass a line of sunken barges out to sea, which helps to reduce erosion, and the sea wall itself becomes more substantial as you approach **Sales Point**.

6 The path deteriorates again to pass a line of benches. Amongst the trees on the right is the Othona Christian Community, which welcomes and involves people of any faith. Arrive at a hide built on stilts.

7 Descend steps and go diagonally right, across the site of a Roman fort, to the **Chapel of St Peter-on-the-Wall**. After exploring the chapel and its surrounds, leave by the track that goes inland to pass through a gate and eventually return to your car.

Cockle Spit Nature Reserve.

Mistley and the Stour Estuary

The Stour Estuary.

Mistley lies at the start of the Stour Estuary and provides views, over hundreds of moored boats, to Suffolk on the other side of the water. It is famous for the particularly nasty exploits of Matthew Hopkins, the self-styled Witchfinder General of the mid 17th century. Along with his assistants, he was responsible for about 100 executions in this area. You will never use the expression 'hangers-on' in the same way after you have read the information board on the side of the Thorn pub.

We pass through woodland with some magnificent old oaks then explore older and very attractive parts of the outskirts of Manningtree before wandering alongside the estuary. It is here that you will encounter two of Mistley's famous sights: the swans – on a good day you may see over 200 of them on the river bank – and later come the Towers – these are the remains of a fine church, the nave of which had to be demolished in the 19th century. Whilst this walk perhaps over-indulges the interests of the walker, streams, meadows, a beach and the woodland will provide plenty of interest for your dog.

Terrain

A mainly level walk with lots of surfaced paths and lush verges. One section through woodland can be muddy.

Where to park

The free car park to the left of Mistley village hall (GR TM122313). Turn off the B1352 at a sharp bend along Shrubland Road to turn left along a narrow drive to the village hall (toilets available). The car park is to the left. **Postcode:** CO11 1FN. **OS map:** Explorer 197 Ipswich, Felixstowe & Harwich.

How to get there

Turn off the A137, which runs between Colchester and Ipswich, near Manningtree station onto the B1352. The road will pass the Towers and then turn inland. Watch for a sharp left-hand bend and turn right here along Shrubland Road. Turn left along a narrow drive to the village hall and the car park.

Nearest refreshments

Rio's Café in the High Street, Manningtree, at the end of point 3 serves breakfasts, lunches and afternoon tea. It is open from 8.30 am to late afternoon 7 days a week. Dogs (well-behaved) and their owners are asked to sit near the door. ☎ 01206 393100. The Mistley Thorn pub at the end of point 4 provides food and drink of a very high order and specialises in fish dishes. Small, well-behaved dogs are welcome. ☎ 01206 392821. www.mistleythorn.co.uk

Dog factors

Distance: 3 miles / 4.8 km.
Road walking: Approximately 340m along pavements through the old town. The walk alongside the estuary is on wide verges.
Livestock: Waterfowl, especially the famous swans. You may encounter cows in the pasture at point 5.
Stiles: 1.
Nearest vets: Highcliff Veterinary Practice, Manningtree.

The Walk

. . . .

1 Walk to the right of the village hall to pick up the left-hand boundary of the playing field towards woodland. Reach a line of concrete fencing posts and go right on a path. Continue along the line of the posts and ignoring side paths, passing some truly magnificent old oaks on the way. Just before the very end of the wood, fork left to a metal kissing gate. Go forward along the field edge with woodland to the left. Cross a stream by an earth bridge at a field boundary and go uphill, alongside metal railings with the Dairy House development on the left to go through another kissing gate. Join a broad track, which soon joins a drive coming in from the left.

2 Keep forward to later swing left. Just past a drive to a house, at the end of a wooden fence, go right at a waymark along an enclosed path with a wire-mesh fence to the right. Join a terrace and continue to a road.

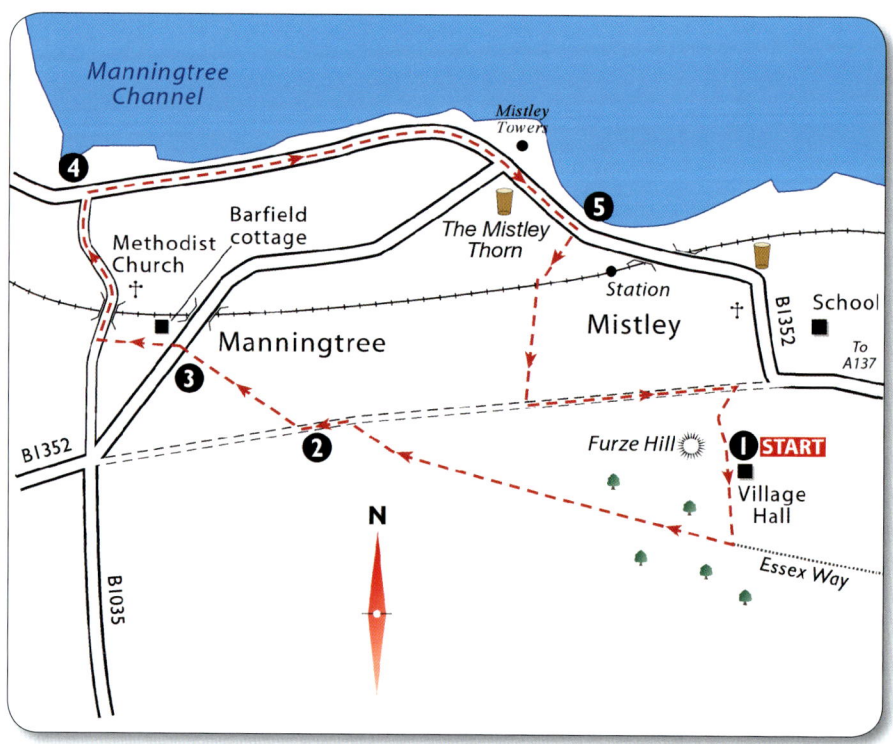

The famous Mistley swans.

3 Cross, taking a path called **Barnfield** to the left of a small garage. Continue along a pathway to the left of **Barnfield Cottage** to reach a road and turn right. Cross the railway and fork right. Go left in front of the Methodist church and continue down **South Street** between a mass of interesting buildings and passing the **Red Lion** to cross the road past **Rio's Café** to reach the riverside.

4 Go right. Quite soon there is a short beach where dogs can have a swim if the tide is in. Later you can wander along a wide grass sward, to arrive at the spot where the famous Mistley swans come to feed. Your dog will be fascinated by the sight of up to 250 swans at high tide and they won't be worried as long as the dog is on a lead. A little further on you will pass **Mistley Towers**. (The **Thorn pub** is across the road on the right, where you can read about the exploits of the Witchfinder General, who was active in this area from 1645 to 1647.) Eventually you will see a large old warehouse on the right.

5 Walk down the right-hand side of the building on the designated walkway, keeping forward to arrive at a metal gate. Go through and turn right, then left up steps to walk through a tunnel under the railway. Go down the other side and keep forward across a meadow. Beyond the first kissing gate you come to an enclosed track and go left. Keep forward, passing a drive coming in from the left and passing houses. At the top of the hill, turn right along a drive signed to the village hall and return to your car.

Wrabness

The woodland is a dog's delight.

It **would be worth** doing this walk for the woodlands alone. Dominated by sweet chestnuts that were probably originally planted by the Romans, they house nightingales, which can be heard in the springtime. During the winter the estuary comes into its own with the vast number of waders that visit the site. Summer visitors will find an abundance of sloes. Harwich Docks are far enough away to be just interesting shapes in the distance – their cranes like a battery of guns pointing to the heavens. Two short diversions visit a fantasy house and a church with its bell on the ground. Once on the ridge you can see for miles on a clear day. Well-behaved dogs can be safely let off the lead for the majority of the walk and they will find the woods full of interest.

Terrain

This is easy walking with a couple of gradual gradients. The route goes through woodland and along field edges.

Where to park

The free car park owned by the RSPB on the edge of the Stour Estuary Nature Reserve, which closes at 7 pm or dusk, whichever is earlier. There is a picnic area here and an information board (GR TM190309). **Postcode:** CO12 5ND. **OS map:** Explorer 197 Ipswich, Felixstowe & Harwich.

How to get there

Follow the A120 towards Harwich from Colchester and turn off towards Wrabness station. Turn right on the B1352; the car park, on the left, will be signed on the right.

Nearest refreshments

There are no cafés or pubs in the immediate vicinity. A good picnic spot is described in stage 3 of the walk, otherwise a trip up the road to Mistley or Manningtree will provide some excellent options.

The Walk

· ·

1 Start the walk by the exit on the left when facing the road. The path swings to the left and there is an immediate fork where you go right. At the next fork go left with a white arrow. Ignore a path to the right, then at the next junction, go right and start following signs to the hides. Climb a short hill, go through a barrier and continue alongside a railway line. After another barrier cross a bridge on the left over the railway and fork left through a barrier and left again to fork right opposite a bench. At the next fork, go left with an arrow. You are now on the **Essex Way** which you will follow for 1½ miles.

Dog factors

· ·

Distance: 4 miles /6.4 km.
Road walking: ⅓ mile along a quiet road.
Livestock: None.
Stiles: 1 – which could be bypassed.
Nearest vets: Kinfauns Veterinary Group, Harwich.

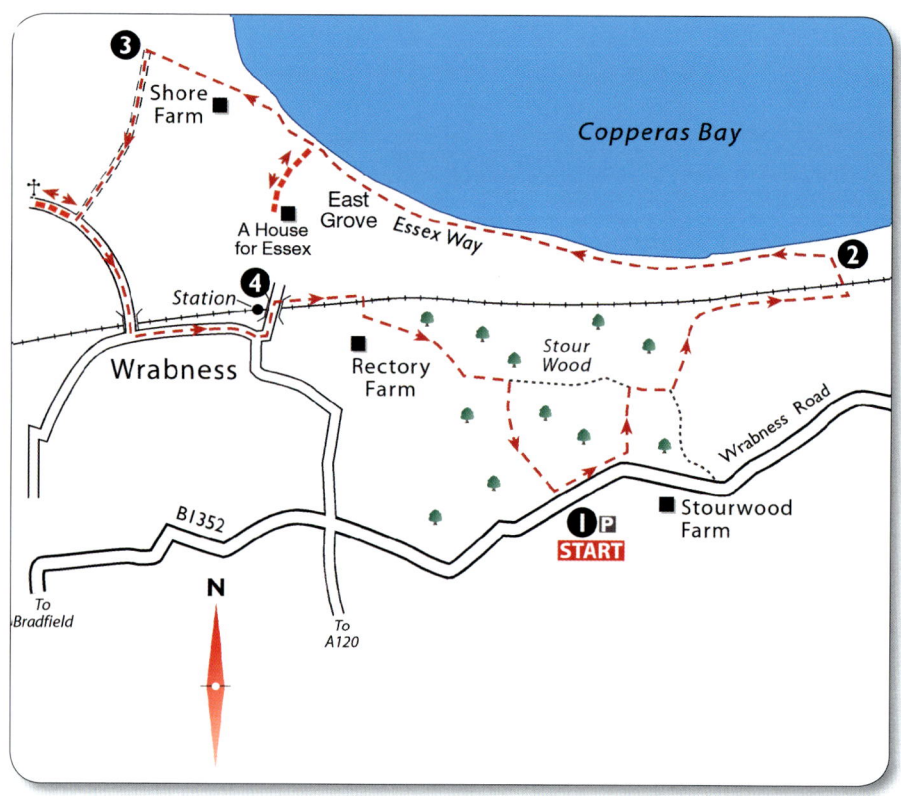

② By now you will be glimpsing the **Stour Estuary** to your right. Follow the poppy signs and keep parallel with the estuary. When you emerge from woodland you will go over a bridge and up some steps. At the end of a long field you join a fenced path and go along the bottom of **Stradlands** garden via deer gates. Keep forward along the lower edge of the next field. When you enter another stretch of woodland, **East Grove**, again keep alongside the estuary, ignoring side paths. Emerge from the woods by a bridge and immediately go left with a fingerpost to Wrabness Shop. Climb gradually to reach A House for Essex. You can walk along two sides of this astonishing building designed by the artist Grayson Perry but it will cost you £1000 to stay a couple of nights. If you are wondering what it's like inside, visit ww.living-architecture.co.uk/the-houses/a-house-for-essex/overview/. Retrace your steps to the **Essex Way** and turn left. Soon you are on another attractive, narrow,

A House for Essex

hedged path, which delivers you right to the edge of the estuary. (Diagonally right you get a good view of the **Royal Hospital School at Holbrook**, across the water in Suffolk.) Pass ShoreFarm on a bank that forms a rudimentary sea wall and continue towards a caravan park.

3 Just before reaching the park, turn left up a broad sandy track. On reaching the road, turn right for a brief visit to the church 200m along the road. (The bell of 11th-century **All Saints' church** fell to the ground in the 17th century when the church's tower collapsed and it has been kept in the graveyard cage ever since.) Retrace your steps and continue along this quiet road as it swings to the right (the information board with its two benches will provide a useful

'Keep up!'.

picnic spot with a fine view of the estuary). Cross the railway and turn left to enter the village of **Wrabness**. (On a corner there is a small but attractive garden with various railway memorabilia.) Cross the road at the corner to continue on **Black Boy Lane**; this takes you across the railway again.

4 Immediately turn right at a fingerpost and emerge from the fenced path to walk on the right field edge. On reaching a bridge on the right, cross the railway for the last time. Go left at waymarkers to follow a clear cross-field path, through a kissing gate, into **Stour Wood**. Keep forward to a track where you go right past a barrier, then left opposite a bungalow. Continue with white and yellow arrows to arrive at a junction with circular trails labelled left and car park right. Go right and stick to this main path to reach your car.

APPENDIX
Veterinary practices located near to the walks

Ark Veterinary Centre
14 Church Lane, Lexden, Colchester CO3 4AF
☎ 01206 572410

Bishop's Stortford Veterinary Hospital
Rye Street, Bishop's Stortford, Hertfordshire CM23 2HA
☎ 01279 654108

Clarendon House Veterinary Centre
Bentalls Centre, Colchester Road, Heybridge, Maldon CM9 4GD
☎ 01621 850124

Companion Care Veterinary Surgery Pets at Home
St James Retail Park, Edinburgh Way, Harlow CM20 2SX
☎ 01279 770104

Edgewood: Purleigh surgery
Chelmsford Road, Purleigh, Chelmsford CM3 6QR
☎ 01621 828381 or 01621 828445

The Forge Veterinary Centre
93b Head Street, Halstead CO9 2AZ
☎ 01787 472666

Goddard Veterinary Group
84 New Wanstead, Wanstead, London E11 2SY
☎ 020 8989 7744

Highcliff Veterinary Practice
Factory Lane, Cattawade, Manningtree CO11 1QL
☎ 01206 391511

House & Jackson
Chevers Pawn, Rookery Road, Blackmore CM4 0LE
☎ 01277 823858

Kinfauns Veterinary Group
14 Oakley Road, Harwich CO12 4QZ
☎ 01255 503807

Medivet, Chafford Hundred
Drake House, Drake Road, Chafford Hundred, Grays RM16 6RX
☎ 01375 480200

Medivet, Maldon Road
St Runwalds Surgery, 94a Maldon Road, Colchester CO3 3AP
☎ 01206 572173

Medivet, Waltham Abbey
15 Sun Street, Waltham Abbey, EN9 1ER
☎ 01992 716771

Mercer & Hughes
Units 5 & 6, Chelmsford Road Industrial Estate, Great Dunmow CM6 1HD
☎ 01371 872836
Devon Lodge, 14 Radwinter Road, Saffron Walden CB11 3JB
☎ 01799 522082/521406

North Weald Veterinary Surgery
42a–44 High Road, North Weald Bassett CM16 6BU
☎ 01992 525556

Rochford Vet Surgery
19 East Street, Rochford SS4 1DB
☎ 01702 545558

Spring Lodge Veterinary Hospital
Spring Lodge Farm, Powers Hall End, Witham CM8 2HG
☎ 01376 513247